PRAISE FOR *CHRISTIANITY AND CLASS WAR*

Very few Christian writers have dedicated a book to the memory Karl Marx, but while Berdyaev pays tribute to 'the social master of his youth' he sees Marxian class war as only the contemporary manifestation of a deeper spiritual struggle. Going further than even the humanist element in Marx could ever go, Berdyaev argues for the rediscovery of work as an authentic spiritual expression of human dignity and worth. It is here—and not by standing aloof from material life—that Christianity must make its voice heard on behalf of those suffering the multiple and catastrophic ill effects of capitalism. Written in the aftermath of the Russian Revolution and in the shadow of impending world war, *Christianity and Class War* is an eloquent call for a creative Christian response to the practical and spiritual challenges of modern society.

— **GEORGE PATTISON**, Honorary Professorial Research Fellow (University of Glasgow)

Readers of this short book, written in 1931 during a time of great upheaval—the rise of the Nazis in Germany, the Great Depression, Stalinism in Russia and the build-up to the Second World War—will be surprised at how relevant this volume is in our age of increasingly sophisticated economic, technological and political control. Nikolai Berdyaev, the author of the book, devoted his entire life and work to the pursuit of truth and the defence of human dignity and freedom. *Christianity and Class War* is an uncompromising critique of secular ideologies on the left and right from a Christian point of view, offering a solution to the materialism and spiritual emptiness of modernity.

— **TSONCHO TSONCHEV**, Ph.D., editor of *The Montreal Review* and a Fellow of the Northwestern University Initiative in Russian Philosophy, Literature and Religious Thought

This small book, written by Berdyaev in the early 1930s at the peak of his creative flourishing, provides a key to understanding his historio-sophical positions and protects the reader from a purely socio-political interpretation of many of the philosopher's statements. Berdyaev offers a Christian anthropological perspective on issues of human rights, the meaning of labour, and the spiritual significance of Economics, which he brilliantly addressed as early as 1918 in his emotive *Philosophy of Inequality*. Here, however, he unfolds his arguments as a comprehensive guide to his philosophy of history and societal life. In 1925, another brilliant Russian philosopher, Fyodor Stepun, who was also permanently exiled from Soviet Russia by the Bolsheviks, criticized Berdyaev, noting that in his *End of Our Time* he does not provide political paths for the embodiment of spiritual potentials outlined in that essay. In this book, Berdyaev exhaustively explains why such political paths do not exist — and what is entailed in his "third way" beyond communism and capitalism, or "right" and "left," stating that he "firmly sits" on this "third chair". Berdyaev clearly demonstrates that bourgeois mentality and economic out-look — the very materialism that turns a person into a thing and labour into a commodity — is, in fact, a spirit. This spirit, he maintains, "cannot be opposed by any economic system" but only by a different spirit.

— **SOFIA ANDROSENKO**, organizer of "Tea with Berdyaev" international meetings (St. Philaret's Institute, Moscow)

CHRISTIANITY AND CLASS WAR

Christianity & Class War

NIKOLAI BERDYAEV

Translated by Donald Attwater
Foreword by Michael Martin

AROUCA
PRESS

Second Edition © by Arouca Press 2025
Foreword © by Michael Martin 2025
Waterloo, ON N2J 0A5
www.aroucapress.com

Kind permission granted by the Attwater
estate to use this translation.
Originally published by Sheed & Ward (New York), 1934.

ISBN: 978-1-998492-47-3 (pbk)
ISBN: 978-1-998492-48-0 (hc)

I dedicate this book to the memory of Karl Marx
who was the social master of my youth and whose
opponent in ideas I have now become.

N. B.

CONTENTS

FOREWORD

Nikolai Berdyaev: A Voice Crying in the Wilderness

MICHAEL MARTIN

I WONDER WHAT HE WAS THINKING, Nikolai Alexandrovich Berdyaev, as he boarded what became known to posterity as the "Philosophers' Ship" as it disembarked from the Soviet Union in September 1922, the cargo of which included some of the most important members of the Russian intelligentsia, Sergei Bulgakov and Semon Frank among them in addition to Berdyaev. Banished from his homeland, the dissident was informed that should he return he would be shot. He was forty-eight years old at the time, one of Russia's most formidable intellectuals and an unapologetic Christian, as idiosyncratic (and borderline heretical) as his Christianity might have been. He had already been arrested and imprisoned several times for his Christian and political views (the two were inseparable for him). He seems to have been almost entirely fearless, and, even though he had been an avowed Marxist in his youth and maintained a vocal critic of capitalism, he knew who the real enemy was. As he writes in his autobiography, "I have remained a spiritual opponent of totalitarian Communism both in Russia and

in the West."[1] The ship travelled to Berlin where Berdyaev
tarried for a short time before leaving for Paris where he
would remain for the rest of his life and where he would
write some of the most radical and prophetic Christian
philosophy ever committed to paper.

To read Berdyaev is to attend to the voice of one crying
out in the wilderness. Born in Kiev in 1874, he spent his
last decades outside of Russia, outside of politics, outside
of the Christian mainstream, yet integral to all of them.
A salon in Paris is the last place one would imagine as his
setting from the absolute and uncompromising wildness
of his ideas and the language in which he couched them.
Though an opponent of the dehumanizing mechanisms
of Marxism and capitalism, in true prophetic form, neither was Berdyaev reluctant to call the Church itself to
repentance; for the failures of the modern world (of which
Marxism and capitalism are but symptoms) are ultimately
failures of the Church and Christians:

> We are witnessing a judgement not on history
> alone, but upon Christian humanity.... The task
> of creating a more just and humane social order
> has fallen into the hands of anti-Christians, rather
> than Christians themselves. The divine has been
> torn apart from the human. This is the basis of
> all judgement in the moral sphere, now being
> passed upon Christianity.[2]

CHRISTIANITY AND CLASS WAR

Christianity and Class War, here published in a
long overdue edition, is both an act of contrition and

---

[1] Quoted in Matthew Spinka, *Nicolas Berdyaev: Captive of Freedom*
(Philadelphia: The Westminster Press, 1950), 65.
[2] Nikolai Berdyaev, *The Fate of Man in the Modern World*, trans.
Donald A. Lowrie (Ann Arbor: The University of Michigan Press,
1935), 118 and 122.

a manifesto, as Berdyaev makes clear in his dedication:

> I dedicate this book to the memory of
> KARL MARX
> who was the social master of my youth
> and whose opponent in ideas I have now become.
>
> N. B.

Berdyaev's primary critique of Marxism in the book resides in the fact that Marxism places the abstract category of "class" above the spiritual reality of the individual man. Christianity does exactly the opposite, which for Berdyaev is the true and proper order. Reading man in terms of class turns the individual into a thing, a cipher, a placeholder for the will-to-power of a system. As such it is spiritually desolate and morally bankrupt; that is, the province of demons.

This is nowhere more obvious than in the Marxist turn from the plight of the worker in the days of Berdyaev to the more recent Marxist iteration as a philosophy (really an academic posture) championing "marginalized groups" (whatever that is supposed to mean) and completely hostile and antagonistic toward the proletariat writ large. This is because terms like "proletariat" and "marginalized groups" represent no reality and are only glittering generalities designed to foment resent and social unrest. As Berdyaev observes, "Marx was a noteworthy master of dialectic who used it for the effective exposition of the class war." Marxism, then, both the variety known by Berdyaev and its current transmogrified iteration, is no philosophy at all but a fluid arrangement of rhetorical propositions that asks only an emotional response. "Class," that is, means nothing. As Berdyaev further argues, "the very existence of classes is a symptom of the change, for

a class is a thing, an object, and not a real being, and
Marxist materialism makes the proletariat believe itself
to be just a lump of matter."

Perhaps Marxism's most fatal blunder is in its gener-
alization of human souls into materialist categories (do
we blame Aristotle?). Indeed, the proletariat as Berdyaev
understood it and the marginalized groups that are pro-
moted today are "made up of men who are like other men,
good and bad, intelligent and dull, noble and base, and,
as in all other classes, the wicked and the stupid predominate." Membership in a class, even a marginalized one,
does not bestow virtue on anyone: "All classes are faulty,
all class psychology is sinful, for they are opposed to the
brotherhood of men; all class isolation is an evil that must
be fought spiritually; and there is nothing more saddening
than to see the sense of sin blunted by class interests and
greed." Marginalized groups are as afflicted by the will-to-
power as any oligarch.

For Berdyaev, the almost invisible hand in the system,
of which Marxism and capitalism are but two willing
servants, is "the mysticism of money." Though Berdyaev
sensed its pervasiveness in the cloak of darkness, in our
own historical moment it conducts its business in the clear
light of day, though bodies such as the European Union
and the World Economic Forum, representing as they do
the perfect marriage between Marxism and capitalism.
The reappearance of this book could not have come at a
better time. In a chilling description as fresh and bracing
as when he wrote it in 1931, Berdyaev explains that the
mysticism of money

> is neither divine nor natural but diabolic, and in
> secret it rules the world. The working classes are
> not the only victims of this phantasmic world,

all suffer from it; man perishes therein and his image is obscured. Contemporary capitalists are haunted by a frantic need for more markets, and they themselves are falling victims to the wild unhuman forces that they serve. They have nothing to hold on to, they cannot stop themselves: their spirit fails, for they can no longer contemplate divine things.

When Berdyaev uses the term "wild unhuman forces" here, he is not employing metaphor. He rightly locates ours as a spiritual battle, "For our struggle is not against flesh and blood, but against the rulers, against the authorities, against the powers of this dark world and against the spiritual forces of evil in the heavenly realms" (Ephesians 6:12).

While I don't know what Berdyaev was thinking as his ship to exile pulled out of the harbor in 1922, I do know what he would think about our situation today—as it always already is the situation of the prophet: "The night is coming and we must take up spiritual weapons for the fight against evil, we must make more sensitive our power for its discernment, we must build up a new knighthood."[3]

Holy Thursday, 2025

---

[3] Nikolai Berdyaev, *The End of Our Time, together with an essay on The General Line of Soviet Philosophy*, trans. Donald Attwater (London: Sheed & Ward, 1935), 119–20.

CHAPTER I

The Class War a Fact • Marx's Theory of Class War

O UR SINFUL WORLD IS THE SCENE
of a conflict between opposed forces: this conflict determines the existence of the organic uni-
verse, it is the central fact of the social world of man, and
would seem also to be carried on in the world of spirits,
good and evil. The whole of cosmic life is dominated by
the principle of polarization, of attraction and repulsion,
and accordingly there is ceaseless warfare. Dialectic is a war
in the order of logic. This universal struggle was seen differently by Heraclitus, by Boehme, by Hegel, by Bahoffen,
by Marx, by Nietzsche, by Dostoievsky. The class war in
the social world is only *one* of the manifestations of this
cosmic struggle and mutual antagonism; it can be seen
also in opposition between the sexes and between nations.

What attitude ought the Christian consciousness to take
up towards this fact? We may each have our own personal
ideas about it, provided only that we must not deny its
existence. It is a Christian duty to look reality in the face
and to keep ourselves fully conscious of it. Nothing is
more unchristian than the "idealization" of reality; it is
precisely the Christian more than anybody else who must
put aside fear whenever the exposure and condemnation

of a horrible and wicked reality is called for. Class war
is an irrefutable fact; it plays a very big part in history,
and our age shows the positive marks of its uncontrolled
violence more clearly than any.

Bourgeois ideologies are not content with trying to hide
this conflict from us but even, generally, go so far as to
deny that there are any classes. In middle-class democratic
societies all men are equal before the law: there are no
class privileges, the poor man can become a millionaire,
the millionaire can become a poor man, juridically and
politically there is no difference between them. We are
therefore entitled to qualify as bourgeois every mind that
believes that the abolition of castes and the conferring of
equality in civil and political rights eradicates oppression,
strife, and social inequality. According to these ideas there
is only an individual conflict, in which victory belongs
not only to the strongest and the luckiest, but equally
to the best and the most useful: it is, in fact, the reward
of certain virtues. The bourgeois mind is optimistic — it
believes in the natural harmony of contradictory interests. Socialists, in the wide sense of the word, seem to be
pessimistic, because our social reality appears to them to
be wicked — and in that respect they are much nearer to
the Christian mind than are the bourgeois.

Even the aristocracy has a certain moral advantage over
the bourgeoisie, in that they honestly and openly recognize inequality and look on themselves as a higher and
privileged order, whereas the bourgeois dissembles his
favoured position: moreover, the patrician does not base
his privileges on the coin of the realm of Mammon. In the
old aristocratic societies classes remained hidden but social
ranks were openly acknowledged, so that it was easy to
detect and condemn their privileges in a way that cannot

be done in a democratic society. Barons' wars were cruel enough but they were undisguised and decent, which is more than can be said for the secret, camouflaged, and elusive warfare that goes on among the banks, stock-exchanges, parliamentary parties, and newspapers of capitalist society. In this society there is a tendency for everything to acquire the character of a complex symbolism, of a secret economic game, of a power belonging to a phantom kingdom of money; this seems to be especially true of the banks, the unseen rulers of the world.

The history of human society is one long exhibition of warfare between various social groups, among races and nationalities, generations and families, religions and sects, schools of thought and practice, trade gilds and professional unions, last of all among social classes, and that, beyond question, is the most cruel strife of all. This endless struggle was recognized long ago by the anarchist Proudhon, and he wrote a vindication of it. The class war was also affirmed by the syndicalist Georges Sorel, but it is Marx who here deserves all our attention for he had a very clear understanding of the desperate warfare that has been kept up by demoniacal and irrational forces through history, and he associated it in an original fashion with an extreme rationalism. But he reduced the manifold conflicts of social groups to the one single class war, as he perceived it in the nineteenth century. He made the categories of western European capitalist society absolute, and then extended them to the whole historical process of the world. But it is only in capitalist society that this antagonism has become in the first place and principally a class war, for classes in the modern sense of the word did not exist in the past. Castes were both a biological and a social phenomenon, biological heredity, the formation of

the natural species, the race, having the principal part. Race
ideologies are always naturalistic.[1] An aristocracy is not a
class in the social sense as we understand it, it is rather
an hereditary breed evolved in the course of centuries;
it is most emphatically not determined by reference to
economic production but by reference to ancestry and its
biological and social inheritance. Class war means the end
of aristocracy, for though it survived strife between races,
nations, and states — by which, indeed, it was formed — it
must succumb in a conflict that is purely social. Aristocracy can have no place in the Marxist scheme.

We have only to put aside all preconceived notions and
look at daily life to see to what an extent the struggle of
classes and social groups really governs the political and
social life of our time. Political parties are almost entirely
determined by class psychology and class interests, and
these parties can be fairly easily classified according to
Marxist categories. When there is a general election or a
political crisis just keep your ears open in what in France
are called *bistros*,[2] in shops and buses, at street corners;
you will keep on hearing such remarks as: "Poincaré is all
right for big business, but Herriot is better for the small
trader." Behind party politics you can always find the
interests of the big financiers, industrialists, and merchants,
of the small capitalists and the ordinary traders, of the
peasants and the industrial workers; it is hardly possible
to find a party that is not conditioned by a social class.
Moreover, mentality and daily life are coloured according

---

[1] Gobineau's theory of races is entirely naturalistic (see his *Essai
sur l'inégalité des races humaines*), and aristocracy justifies itself by
naturalistic rather than social arguments; see Bouglé's *La Démocratie
devant la Science*.
[2] And in England "pubs." [TR.]

to the class concerned; there are radical differences of temperament and conditions of life between the aristocracy and the bourgeoisie, between the upper, middle, and lower middle-class, between the professional classes and the "intellectuals." The existence of mentalities peculiar to the official class and to the *intelligentzia* is a difficulty in the application of Marx's theory, because these social groups cannot be determined with reference to production.

There can also be particular groups, products of exceptional circumstances, which have a common mentality, a public opinion, and a mode of life proper to them. Such an one is the Russian "emigration," of which the greater part is drawn from classes which in the past were privileged. Its social composition is complex, for it includes representatives of the nobility, of all the degrees of upper and middle officialdom, of the commercial and industrial bourgeoisie, and of intellectuals of varied occupations and views; peasants and industrial workers are very few. This body has its own specific tendencies, and class judgements of the revolution and Soviet Russia predominate. It is not easy for these *émigrés*, even for those with democratic and radical tendencies, to understand that opinions about Sovietism can differ radically, accordingly as they come from members of the former privileged classes who have been maltreated and ruined under the communist regime or from representatives of the new Russia, who have been called from among the toiling masses to help build up the new state and have, in consequence, profited from Communism. One part of the emigration, particularly its younger members, has in fact been turned into a working-class which is socially a real proletariat; but very many of these workers have nevertheless kept the psychology and outlook of the nobility and look on themselves as belonging to a favoured social rank which, for the time being, is in difficulties. Some of these young *émigrés* who work in factories have learned to loathe the capitalist system, but this does not prevent them from being still traditional monarchists, nationalists, and children of the privileged classes. From this example we can get a good idea of the complexity of the formation and psychology of such social groups.

Although his scheme presented this state of things in a simplified form, Marx nevertheless detected a profound truth in it. Revolutions have a class character just as much as has ordinary political life. In the history of revolutions, whatever symbolism they adopt, under whatever standard of ideas they gather, it is always oppressed and enslaved classes revolting against privileged and governing classes; there is always an emergence from the collective subconsciousness of the people of a demand for compensation for their heaped-up grievances and for the humiliations they have undergone. Class revenge plays a leading part in every revolution; there is always a social turning-upside-down in which the high are brought low and the low exalted. The symbolism of Liberty, Equality, and Fraternity or of Marxist Communism is in a way only a banner hoisted in the midst of the battle of social classes.

Marxists maintain that there can be such a thing as "class-truth" because they have not followed their reasoning to its conclusion, for actually it is impossible to make this affirmation real in thought. The hypothesis that truth can be the reflection of the economic reality and social state of any class is a fundamental contradiction and gnoseological absurdity of Marxism; such a supposition makes knowledge impossible, it is equivalent to a denial of the theory of economic materialism, and so destroys the very foundation of Marxism.

What, in fact, is at the bottom of the materialist conception of history? Is it only the fleeting reflection of the condition of the working-class under the capitalist system and a practically useful weapon in the struggle? Or does it represent the *truth* about the nature of society and the historical process, which, being truth, must be absolute?

Marx would never allow that his theory was relative or rank it with those others that reflect an economic reality and voice the interests and psychology only of a class: he was the bearer of a revelation touching the mystery of the historical process. Now in principle there are no such things as absolute truths, but in reality there is at least one, namely, that there is no absolute truth, and that all truth is only a reflection of economics and the class-war! But this doctrine lifts the knowing subject above all relativity. It would seem that the proletariat whose truth Marx expounded has a cognitive superiority over all other classes; its consciousness is no longer the illusive ideological reflection of economics but is open to the knowledge of reality. This problem preoccupied me a great deal in my youth; I was a Marxist at that time and was writing my first book, *Subjectivism and Individualism in Social Philosophy*. I even tried to construct a proletarian gnoseology. But as I was never a materialist I could not be an orthodox Marxist: philosophically I was an idealist, and when I got over Schopenhauer I nurtured myself on the theories of Kant and Fichte. I looked on truth, goodness and beauty as absolutes, for I had seen that they are rooted in transcendental consciousness and that only the degrees in which we apprehend them are relative. The whole question lies in knowing what conditions of psychological consciousness are favourable to the revelation of transcendental truth. I believed that the proletariat, in as much as it is a hard-working and unified class, exploited and itself innocent of the sin of exploitation, has a psychical structure that is favourable for this revelation, that its psychological consciousness, so to say, coincides with transcendental consciousness. I merely found its social and psychological conditions favourable to the apprehension of absolute truth, logical, though not psychological, and also favourable to the struggle for the good in the ethical sense. I did not express this in terms of orthodox Marxist philosophy but it corresponded well with the *pathos* of Marxian socialism and the idea of the great mission of the proletariat. Later on I departed far from the ideas of my youth, but I continued to regard as fundamental the problem that is raised by the relation between human and supra-human knowledge, the question of the absoluteness of known truth: that is, the problem of the conditions that are humanly favourable to the knowledge of truth.

Truth cannot belong to one single class, but it can be perverted by a class, and history shows that in fact it often has been. Marx was certainly right when he asserted that there was class-falsehood in capitalist society, that it disseminated lies and illusions. The whole of his sociology is a social pathology, but his social physiology was at fault; he was obsessed and distracted by the diseased conditions of capitalist society, and could see no healthy evolution beyond it. According to him, health, that is, the socialist collectivity of the future, had to be the result of the shocking state of the proletariat under Capitalism, things had to get worse and worse in order that they might be better (*Verelendungstheorie*).

Nevertheless, the current notion that the class war was invented by Marx and the socialists, and that it is carried on solely by the revolutionary workers, is dishonest and wrong; it is actually carried on just as much by the middle and governing classes. But when its object is to maintain existing and privileged conditions it has a less aggressive aspect than when it is directed towards changing the actual social regime: in other words, the maintenance of the *status quo* is not looked upon as an arbitrary act of war, but to try to alter it is. That is one of our contemporary fallacies.

Inasmuch as the workers and socialists wage their class war openly, declaring publicly that they are fighting for the proletarian cause, to improve their position, to increase their power, they are superior to the bourgeois who are doing the same thing but under the cover of lofty sentiments: they appeal to patriotism, the safety of the State, liberty, the principles of civilization, and, most unhappily, to religion. In political and social life idealistic shadows, self-suggestion, and other illusions too often blind us to realities; that which is consciously experienced is far from agreeing with that which moves us subconsciously. The method of Marx can be approximated to that of Freud: he denounces the deceptions of consciousness and exposes the impulses and inclinations that lie below in the subconsciousness of the classes; but his rationalist psychology prevents him from going deeply enough into what he finds. In the end what remains of his (and still more his successors') work is a crude libel in which the bourgeois classes are accused of deliberately criminal intentions.

In reality it is irrational forces rather than human greed that are at work in history. Lofty notions and the rhetoric that goes with them most certainly play a treacherous and deadly part in social life, but it does not follow that the holders of these ideas are consciously deceitful or that they are necessarily led by interested motives. When falsehood has once been legitimated, all those who make use of it appeal to the law, which is accordingly often made to shelter injustice. Although it has bred new fallacies, Marxism must at any rate be given the credit of having insisted on social realism and the facing of facts, of having looked at history in the first place as a collision between opposites, and of having refused to believe in ideas that have no driving-power behind them. Marxism upsets sentimental social idealism; it sees all life as determined by a correlation of forces. The Marxist theory of Being is false, for it finds it only in material processes and does not perceive its fundamental principles, it does not know the primary source of all power; but it must be recognised that a large part of Marxian criticism is true and much of its denunciation justifiable. Ideas, principles, norms, are useless by themselves, and it is no good opposing Marxism with them; the only adequate weapon is Being, and deeper and stronger being than that on which Marxism itself rests.

In the ultimate analysis Marxism is a lie, because there is an omnipotent power which is the fount of all power, God. It cannot be denied that social life is controlled by power, but neither economics nor class war is the supreme might; that can be found only in the spirit — even the strength of sin is spiritual. Matter is weak, inert, passive; spirit is active, it moves the very materialists who refuse to recognize it. There is nothing more absurd than to base actuality on a materialist philosophy. Being is not determined by consciousness, but consciousness by being; but being is spirit, not matter, which is only a construction of consciousness.

It is perfectly true that academic idealism and juridical liberalism are powerless. Law can express and rely on force alone, but this force is not economic power, which is not so deeply rooted; moreover, the psychological structure of economics is very complex, and its process cannot be identified with the material process. Economics is a creation of the human spirit, its quality is determined by the spirit, its basis is spiritual;[3] the conditions of economic development are not solely material and physical but integrally psychical. Classes are not necessarily guided by interests that are consciously economic: only a rationalist and eudaemonist psychology could assert such a thing; the emotions of a class mentality are quite capable of producing actions that are foolish and prejudicial for that class. Marxism, it is true, emphasizes the distinction between class interests and personal interests; when a class thinks, expresses its will, and acts in accordance with its own interests, personality may well be destroyed, for it is only a tool in the hands of the class.

It is thus that Marxists explain what they call the imperialist wars to which capitalism gives birth. But the madness of a war provoked by demoniacal irrational forces is inexplicable in the light of the materialist theory of class war or of an economic standpoint or interest. The world war of 1914–18 was a terrible, even a mortal, blow to capitalism, and opened the way to communism, which ought to be accordingly grateful to it. Here the rational scheme of Marxism does not correspond with the irrational reality. It is beyond question that the last war was bred by the insanity and unreasonableness of the capitalist regime, but it does not follow that it was in the economic interests of the capitalist classes — on the contrary. Communists

---

[3] This has been sufficiently shown in the works of Max Weber, Sombart, and Tröltsch.

anathematize the carnage which gave them birth and determined their psychical structure; they pretend indignation against the new war to be hatched by the bourgeoisie, when all the time they want it, knowing that it would mean a definite victory for themselves.

All this shows the psychological complexity of Marxism. Marxists are generally bad psychologists; they do not understand the mentality of the different classes, and their explanations of them are elementary exercises in rationalism and utilitarianism. In short, a true psychology of social classes has yet to be created.[4]

The Marxist theory of classes breaks with the old idea of "the people" and strikes hard both at "popularism" and at conventional democracy. The sovereign people is broken up into classes, whose interests are opposed and which fight each other fiercely. To Rousseau's democratic myth of the sovereign people Marx opposes the socialist myth of the proletariat, a messianic class feigning to voice the general will and called to bring freedom and salvation to mankind. Although it is manifestly mythological and an unconscious revival of the old idea of Israel as the chosen people of God, nevertheless the Marxist doctrine of class war is more closely related to reality than that of Rousseau on the general will and the infallibility and sovereignty of the people. Marx transferred infallibility from the people to the proletariat, but it exists no more in the one than in the other.

In every people or nation which has assumed the form of democracy there is indubitably class war, and the "general will" of the people is a conventional fiction. There are, of course, national and state interests which transcend

---

[4] De Man tried to do it; see his *Au delà du Marxisme.*

the classes and which must be protected if society is to live, and class power is called on to safeguard at least a minimum of these interests. But a democracy, formally understood, hides the actual strife among parties and frequently becomes an instrument whereby one class exercises predominant power: a political masquerade. This can be seen particularly in France, where the parties go so far as to bear fictitious names; one that is in no sense socialist will call itself that at election-time in order to get more votes. Parliament is supposed to represent the will of the people; it is in reality a battlefield of parties whose smoke and din obscures another battle — of classes. Thus the vital interests of the "working people" do not get a chance, and they are, in fact, looked after only by the trade unions. So far in history democracy has been formal and not real, and in that respect the criticism made by Marxists and even by communists seem to me well founded. Democracy gives political rights to a man without giving him the means to profit by them, for the possibility to do so belongs to the social and economic, and not to the political sphere.

In political democracies men are very easily reduced to unemployment, neediness, indigence; the individual's economic rights are not guaranteed to him and the possession of electoral rights is no help at all. Political and juridical equality go hand in hand with the greatest social and economic inequality; social ranks may be done away with and all citizens declared on a level, but the disaggregation of society into classes reaches its maximum. There is the real condemnation of the myth of equality to which the French Revolution gave currency, and it is France which gives characteristic examples in which the phenomenon can be examined in all its purity. In a democracy based on universal suffrage and parliamentarism the nation is organized by the State, but society is not; its organization parallel to the state produces very great difficulties, which lead to social disintegration. Society was incontestably stronger in pre-revolutionary France.

It is impossible to make a stand against a democratic state founded on the myth of the sovereign people; I must repeat that the only real social organizations are the trade unions. A real democracy must be social, industrial, and economic, giving effect to the interests and proper needs of all sorts of work and of people. Marxian criticism is amply justified, but Marxism in its turn has created a new proletarian mythology, and that too puts fictions in the place of realities. It is a new and fanatical form of infallibility, and it cannot be allowed, for authentic infallibility is a spiritual enlightening and transfiguration of man and of nature.

CHAPTER II

Criticism of Marx's Theory • Society & Class •
Class Regarded from the Point of View of Worth

A S WE HAVE ALREADY SEEN, MARX
made the categories of the capitalist regime absolute and extended them beyond the economy of
his own age; he thought he could see a conflict between
the "proletariat" and the "bourgeoisie" throughout the
whole of history, although, in fact, these classes were not
always in existence.

The term "bourgeoisie" is used equivocally in Marxism,
and is given very different meanings. On the one hand,
it is applied to a class which arose under capitalism and
which is determined by reference to a particular mode of
economic production; on the other, it designates the whole
of the controlling class, whose members have always been
exploiters and well endowed with material goods. The
bolshevists prefer to use the word in the second sense, so
that all classes, including intellectual workers and excepting
the proletariat, are assigned to the bourgeoisie. Thus the
word loses its real meaning and becomes a symbol.

But Marx's conception of the bourgeoisie was equiv-
ocal in another sense as well. It represented the class of
exploiters, of "blood-drinkers" who are set against the final

development of society and so bound to perish, but it also
meant for him the class which had the great positive mission of developing productive material forces and bringing
about conditions which would allow the future triumph of
socialism, without which the messianic class, the proletariat
itself, could never exist. Capitalist industrialism is a good
thing, for its factory system has been responsible for the
organization of the workers. In one aspect of his social
theory Marx was an evolutionist, which accounts for the
stages of development in his opinions, but this evolutionist element has disappeared entirely among the Russian
communists, who do their best to make the war between
proletariat and bourgeoisie independent of the existence
of capitalism; for them, the two classes are symbols rather
than realities. In fact, the proletariat is a negligible fraction
of the Russian people, and the bourgeoisie, always a small
body, has now, to all intents and purposes, ceased to exist.
Russian communists do not regard the future communist
society as a product of the development of capitalism but
as a result of "constructivism," the consciously-directed
efforts of the almighty Soviet power; the rule of "necessity"
has given place to the rule of "liberty," a radical change-
over. Such is the metamorphosis that the Marxian idea
has undergone.

For Marx the doctrine of the class war is separate from
capitalism, a reflection or symptom of its reality — so
at least aver those Marxists who claim to be scientific.
Marx was given to thinking in antitheses, which, with
him, assume an universal and absolute character; the
fundamental antinomy, for example, of the bourgeoisie
and the proletariat, of capitalism and socialism, embraces
the whole of life; it covers opposition between different
types of culture, religion, philosophy, morals, as well as

that which is social and economic. The proletariat and atheism are one, the bourgeoisie and religion are one: the first implies materialism and collective morality, the second implies idealism, spirituality, and individual virtue; and so on.

This universalizing of antitheses arises from Marx's monistic economic metaphysic. Actually, the opposition of "communist Russia" to "capitalist Europe" has only a relative and partial meaning from the social and economic standpoints, and can in no sense be said to be universal. Just as Europe is not solely capitalistic (for it contains elements which capitalism cannot account for), so Soviet Russia has numerous aspects, and is far from being solely communistic. There are currents of philosophy and theology, for example, in contemporary western Europe which it would be stupid to look on as favourable to capitalism: Thomism is, to a certain extent, hostile to it; there is the philosophy of Max Scheler, the school of Karl Barth favours socialism, and the religious socialism of Tillich even sympathizes with communism. All these tendencies are strictly anti-materialist, and the religious movements are more hostile to capitalism and the bourgeois spirit than are any others. Heidegger's philosophy does not choose between capitalism and socialism, and is so detached that only those obsessed by economic materialism can seriously call it capitalist. So far, economic materialism has achieved only wretchedly poor results in its attempts to explain philosophical and spiritual ideas and tendencies; Marx himself, who had acute penetration of mind, was wise enough to abstain from going into detailed explanations and so avoided these feeble banalities.

The logical structure of Marxism is flatly contradictory and philosophically childish so far as the class war is

concerned. Marx held to an extreme scholastic realism in
his concepts; he took the abstractions of thought for the
realities of being. To take into consideration the whole
of a society and its culture and then to characterize it as
capitalist and bourgeois *in its entirety* is to abstract from
and hypostasize concepts, and it is just the same with the
notion of the proletariat as a universal class. Lenin recognized that there can be no such thing as a proletarian
culture, and that the proletariat can only share and absorb
a culture that is already existing. We shall see presently
that the fundamental logical error into which, it seems to
me, Marx fell was the confusion of extreme realism with
extreme nominalism.

It is impossible to determine the concept of a class
or social group from the economic point of view alone,
with reference to production only, as Marx wanted to
do: social differentiation is effected by other things and
conditioned by other principles as well. History is full of
the conflicts of social groups which had been formed by
numerous factors and modified by different sides of life,
religious, national, intellectual groups, and others. These
groups were already face to face in primitive societies
wherein economic classes in the Marxian sense did not
exist. Totemistic beliefs determined the social system of a
tribe and fashioned its unity: the bond of totem-kinship
was closer than that of blood.[1] Simmel's theory of social
differentiation and of the forming and mixing of groups is
considerably deeper, more complex, and subtler than that
of Marx.[2] The castes of India do not fit into the Marxian
scheme and are unexplainable on a basis of class war, for

---

[1] See Durkheim's *Les formes élémentaires de la vie religieuse.*
[2] See Simmel's *Soziologie.*

they were determined by a religious idea. The "intellectuals" are another, not merely group, but whole social class, which Marxism does not account for; obviously they can subserve capitalism, flatter the middle-classes, and create a bourgeois ideology, but they belong to the bourgeoisie no more than they do to the proletariat.

I remember a characteristic example of the sort of thing that happens under Sovietism. The Russian Writers' Society was to register among the other professional associations so as to be able properly to look after its members' interests, but it could not be done because the creative work of literature had no place in the Soviet-Communist scheme of things, a scheme which envisages only work that bears more or less directly on economic production. And so, as writers are not producers of material goods, they had to register themselves as printers! The intellectuals do not come within the category of social classes, they are looked on solely as a group which is at the service of the bourgeoisie or of the proletariat, of capitalism or of communism. Curiously enough, their economic situation is actually the most precarious and insecure of any in the world; they are outcasts, the least organized of any workers, and at times of crisis their creative activity is thrown aside as a useless luxury. Marx refused to admit that social groups are formed not only in the spheres of productive work but also in those where creative activities are of a purely spiritual and intellectual nature.

He attributed an absolute significance to "class," and it has certainly played a very big part in history, but its importance is relative, it is a constituent but not an integral part of man. The most striking and unhuman error of Marxism consists in refusing to see man above the classes but to place classes above man, to reduce man in

his highest manifestations and his deepest spiritual expe-
riences to a subordinate function of the class which must
condition both his contemplation and his creative work.
Marx repudiated the permanent value of *homo economicus*,
of "bourgeois political economy"; he made of that value a
mere historical category, and provided communist society
with the vision of a completely new man. But his theory
of class war and economic materialism itself involves, in so
far as it is a universal explanation of mankind and society,
a making absolute of this "economic man." The conscious
methodological abstraction exercised by classical political
economy is transformed by him into a concrete doctrine
of man and of human nature in general. Adam Smith
recognized the existence of man moved by moral sympathy
alongside of economic man moved only by self-interest,
and devoted a special treatise to the study of him from
this aspect. A considerable number of abstract doctrines,
based on one principle or another, can be formulated
about man (and each one is legitimate), accordingly as he is
considered as a religious being *par excellence*, as a political
animal, as *homo faber*, as a creature having reason, or as
a sick person who must be healed.[3] I shall return later to
the problem of "man and class."

From the point of view of logic the whole theory of
class war is contradictory and vicious for, as I have already
said, there is nothing so childish and uncritical as Marx's
logic, which affirms simultaneously an extreme logical
realism in regard of class and a no less extreme nominalism in regard of society, which, according to him, would
become real only when it became socialist. Throughout

---

[3] See my book, *De la destination de l'homme: Essai d'éthique
paradoxale.*

the whole of pre-socialist history, society is conceived from an "atomic" standpoint, as a battlefield of classes moved by opposing interests; it is an aggregation of material atoms reciprocally attracted within their classes and reciprocally repulsed outside them. This gross materialism is mitigated and complicated by a dialectic borrowed from Hegel, a loan which was not effected without great sacrifice of logic. There cannot be a dialectical development in society unless there is a real integration within which the dialectical process can be accomplished, and this it is impossible to envisage from the materialist point of view, for materialism is atomistic and nominalist.

The class war is carried on within society, which itself constitutes a certain initial unity and reality in advance of the classes which compose it, and it is only by admitting this that positive and valuable results may be expected from the class war. In fact, if there is no such thing as society, and classes alone are real, then their conflict can end only in definitive disintegration. The dialectic of the class war upon which Marx insists so strongly assumes the triumph of common sense and right reason throughout society and mankind at large. But no integration, much less judgement and reason, is conceivable as the result of a conglomeration of heterogeneous elements; judgement and reason have to rise above these elements, and that means that society must have a greater reality than class, though that class, too, is real must not be denied in consequence of this. The life of an organism cannot consist wholly of diseased processes, for these necessitate the existence of healthy physiological phenomena which are indispensable for the conservation of life itself. There is a physiology of social life parallel to the pathology of class war and its violence, injustice, and perversion of truth.

While Marx, in his affirmation of the reality of the class, on I don't know what logical foundation, disproves the reality of society, he also denies that of personality: they are both a function of class, that unity and integration from which both receive their being and all their life. Man has no interior nature but is in essence an economic creature dependent on a class. But while society is called upon to become a reality in its socialist future, personality, according to Marx, has never been a reality, and presumably never will be. He associates nominalism and atomism with universalism in a most astonishing way; the sovereign reality of class asserts itself and must then be transformed into the universal reality of the social "collective." On the higher level, society is a function of class; on the lower level, personality is such a function: class is, in a way, the substance, the *noumenon*, the thing-in-itself, and everything else is only accident.

But can class be conceived as this unique and original reality? Marx made a mythology of it, which was not at all justified by his materialist notion of the world; materialistically speaking, a class is only a collection of individual atoms struggling to maintain their own interests, atomic men bound to one another by their common economic interests and their relationship with material production. Class as a whole, coming before its parts and determining their life, as a unity and original reality, exists in the mind but not in being; therefore it should be considered organically and not mechanically. An organism is distinguished from a mechanism in this, that it precedes and determines its parts; in a mechanism it is the reverse. But it is not a habit of the materialist mind to think of anything as a whole, and when Marxists maintain that their materialism is dialectical and not mechanical they affirm a logical monstrosity, namely, the union of dialectic and materialism. Hegel turns in his grave and Plato is shocked among the shades. If you are materialists, it is no good pretending to be dialecticians; you are the base-born of Helvetius and Holbach, brothers to Buchner and Moleschott. "Dialectical materialism" is all right for demagogy but not for philosophy, who is an aristocrat. It was in spite of his materialism that Marx was a noteworthy master of dialectic who used it for the effective exposition of the class war.

In the empirical reality of capitalist society we can see various kinds of workmen distinguished from one another by their mentalities and their interests: printers differ greatly from miners. National types, too, are radically different, as, for example, Englishmen organized into trade unions and Germans grouped within the social-democratic party. The industrial and financial bourgeoisie also shows a great variety, and, in fact, this diversity of psychical build is to be found everywhere. The very system of economics is modified considerably by national psychological characteristics, as in France, where industrial backwardness is in a great degree due to the Frenchman's carefulness with money and unwillingness to take risks. It is indeed impossible to find in empirical reality any such single and integral proletariat as was conceived by Marx; it is a fabric built in the mind, an idea, a myth, but, like all significant myths, not completely unrelated to a reality. There is less foundation, however it is looked at, for seeing class as an organic reality than for so seeing society or personality. Class is simply a function of the social process, and everything to do with it is only a constituent part of society, subordinate to personality, and not the reverse.

Here we reach Marx's biggest contradiction. He demonstrates that capitalism turns relations of men into relations of things. That is his most notable discovery and an authentic truth. But it signifies that beyond the economic and material world Marxism perceives living men and creative beings, that it appreciates their energy and their work. The economic process is the struggle of living creatures and constitutes their creative activity. There is no substantial economic reality; consequently, all economic categories are only historical categories, and not eternal principles as the classical bourgeois political economy teaches.

But such an interpretation of economic life is in radical contradiction with materialism, for it is precisely materialism that turns men into things. The treatment of man only as a material object and of his work as a commercial commodity was brought about by the materialist spirit in capitalism. This state of things cannot be opposed by materialism, but must be met by a personal system which sees living subjects as such, and will not allow them to be reduced to the status of means and objects. It is not a class but personality which revolts against this transformation, and the proletarian class in particular pushes it to even further extremes; indeed, the very existence of classes is a symptom of the change, for a class is a thing, an object, and not a real being, and Marxist materialism makes the proletariat believe itself to be just a lump of matter. Marxism is a revolt against capitalism, but it has been bred by it and carries the fatal mark of its materialist spirit. It says that human personality is a function of class, and class in its turn is a function of economic production, so that reality is not constituted by living men but by the productive economic process. It is the Christian conception of the world, and not the materialist, which is in opposition to this transformation of men into things, and this metamorphosis of human beings, which is brought about in the name of a class or of the development of productive material forces, can be combatted only in the name of man. But man is wanting in the Marxism of the past and the present. Shall we find him there in the future?

No; there will only be a completely socialized and completely rationalized human creature. There will be nothing personal and irrational left about him, nothing in him impervious to society and to rationality, no longer a man but something new produced by the class war. But for the birth of a new man, really a man, it is necessary that he should have existed in the past and lived as a deeper reality than any mere class. A "class-ape" can never evolve into a human man.

The future is fundamentally different from the past in Marxist consciousness; the past is the introduction to that "super-history" which will follow the end of history. The past was ruled by necessity, the future will be ruled by liberty; the past was determined by an irrational economic process of which social man had not yet made himself the master, the future will be determined by organized social rationality; between the one and the other there is a great gulf fixed (*Zusammenbruch*). Marx assigns not economic materialism but panlogism as the philosophy for the socialist era which the proletariat is to usher in; socialized man will subdue the irrational forces in nature and society; life will everywhere be strictly controlled and organized and will no longer be dependent on those irrational powers as in all previous societies; the class war and the dialectical social process will end in the triumph of rationality. Necessity will give birth to freedom.

There is nothing more contradictory and paradoxical than this synthesis in Marx of rational and irrational elements, and in Soviet actuality this paradox takes on flesh and lives. Though the Russian communists boast of being orthodox Marxists they do not determine politics by economics, but the contrary. This has often been pointed out by the menshevists,[4] who also call themselves orthodox Marxists. But the communists are more faithful to another element of Marxism, which is turned towards the future. In the past, politics were always conditioned by economics, that is, by unorganized and irrational elemental forces; in the future, the reverse will take place: in other words, organized social rationality will govern the world. Russian communists think that they are already in this future and enjoying the rule of liberty. The Central Committee of the Communist Party is the organ of panlogism, it is social rationality incarnate. But will the success of the proletariat, the abolition of classes, the establishment of this organized rationality be a victory for man? He was borne down in the past by classes and class warfare. Will he survive in the future?

No. He will definitively disappear, leaving only a "collective" behind him. Hegel's philosophy long ago presented us with a marked anti-personalism, and this was taken over by Marxism. The proletariat is no longer content to be a class, it must be the one and only mankind. That is the final result of a class war waged on behalf of the oppressed and exploited. And that brings us to the very heart of Marxism and its theory of classes.

Marx watched the antagonism between the classes of the capitalist society in which he lived; his observations thereon are often perfectly just and he was the first to draw certain true conclusions therefrom, though the French

---

[4] Socialist opponents of the bolshevists. [TR.]

historians Thierry and Guizot and others had already written of class war. But at the same time his proletarian theory was not scientific but religious, messianic, mythical; he created the myth of the messiah-proletariat, the unique class free from the original sin of exploitation, the elect people of God, saviours of mankind, endowed with every virtue. This myth belongs to a very different plane from that on which the empirical class war is actually carried on.

The proletariat is assuredly the most oppressed and outcast class of capitalist society, and therefore especially calls for sympathy and deserves in justice to be released from its burden. But this is not equivalent to a guarantee of its virtue: it is made up of men who are like other men, good and bad, intelligent and dull, noble and base, and, as in all other classes, the wicked and the stupid predominate. The very fact of its numerical superiority carries with it a certain proportion of evil. There never has been and there never will be such a thing as a "good class": it is not classes but men who are good, intelligent, and noble, and they are these things precisely in the measure that they get outside their class and overcome its limitations. All classes are faulty, all class psychology is sinful, for they are opposed to the brotherhood of men; all class isolation is an evil that must be fought spiritually; and there is nothing more saddening than to see the sense of sin blunted by class interests and greed.

The Marxian idea of the proletariat does not necessarily conform to the proletariat as it really is: the portrait which it draws does not, in fact, bear much resemblance to the empirical working-class which it professes to represent; there is a certain likeness in the economic features, but none at all in the spiritual. It is just here that Marx ceases to be a materialist and becomes an extreme idealist; being

no longer determines consciousness, but the "consciousness" of Marx determines the "being" of the proletariat.
His teaching about the proletariat, which is at the centre
of all the class-war theory and controls the conception of
the other classes, appertains strictly to a doctrine of worth
(axiology); the distinction he makes between the proletariat
and the bourgeoisie corresponds to the distinction between
good and evil, light and darkness, superiority and inferi-
ority. If it had not been for this moment of reference to
worth, Marx would never have reached his conception of
the classes, which he always considers in terms of valuation.
Theoretically and in his speech he was an immoralist, but
in reality he was permeated by an excessive moralism which
is apparent throughout his theory of the class war; he
saw in the antagonism of proletariat and bourgeoisie the
struggle between Ormuz and Ahriman. To a fundamental
monism he joined a fundamental dualism.

But the doctrines of worth of Marx and of Christianity
are diametrically opposed. He did not confine himself
to the statement of a war among classes drunk with malice and hate; he rejoiced at the sight and hailed it as a
supremely good thing, because it would necessarily lead on
to the triumph of the messiah-class which, thanks to this
war, would rationalize the whole of life. All his materialism,
his atomism, his nominalism disappear, and give place to
another Marx, who is an idealist, a panlogist, a moralist,
a man of religion and a maker of myths. His conception
of class is only a scientific disguise; it is the axiological
idea that is the decisive influence. He was obsessed by
the facts of exploitation and of the conflict between the
exploited and their exploiters, but the inference that he
deduced therefrom was neither scientific nor economic:
it was axiological and ethical. He tried to make the fact

of exploitation clear by means of the theory of surplus-value, which he took to be purely economic, although it contains an effective ethical element which determines it. Exploitation roused Marx to indignation and censure. But for what reason? Why is exploitation blameworthy and why should it be condemned?

Without any doubt Marx here starts from an ethical premise, from which he concludes that exploitation is an evil and a sin, even the greatest evil and the worst sin. He could not reach this ethical premise scientifically or borrow it from economics. The problem of the class war is not solely social and economic, it is also, and must be, ethical; but the two elements must be distinguished. Now Marx's theory of surplus-value and the class war is a mixture of the two notions: economics are "ethicized" and ethics are "economized." But his moralism is perverted, even demoniacal: he looks on evil as the only highway towards good, an increase of darkness is the only means of getting light; brotherhood, equality, and friendship among men are born out of envy, hatred, malice, and all uncharitableness, violence and repression bring freedom in their train. In some dialectical way iniquity changes into goodness, dark into light; the mischiefs of capitalist society must get worse and worse so that the glories of socialist collectivity may be established.

For the mythology of liberty, equality, and fraternity Marx substituted the messianic proletariat. He was unable to see the real proletariat in all its complexity of good and bad, strength and weakness, but sought to create one anew and so to reveal the power of the myth-idea (contradictory though that is to materialism), and in a considerable measure he was successful. That is his importance in the history of social thought and achievement. Nevertheless,

he did not understand that the "working-man" can quite
easily become a bourgeois and that subconsciously he
is moved by middle-class ideas and instincts, as the history of the European socialist and labour movements has
abundantly proved. The opposition of the working-class
and of Socialism to the middle-classes and their spirit is
exceedingly relative; strictly speaking, there has been no
such opposition except at the time when revolutionary
dreams had not yet attained maturity. At the present day
it does not exist among European socialists, especially
the German social-democrats, who persist in esteeming
themselves Marxists. The anti-bourgeois spirit is shown
only by the communists, and even with them it will be
only for a time; Communism is a new growth of the revolutionary spirit which has appeared on the fertile ground
of the World War, but this spirit also is feeling the attraction of a middle-class greed for power and comfort. The
working-man quite definitely wants to become bourgeois,
and it is necessary from the social point of view to admit
his right to do so. It is not the workers but a number of
intellectuals and other representatives of a high degree of
culture who show a strong aversion from the bourgeois
spirit, and these live in the hope of seeing a new era in
which they will be delivered from it.

Henri de Man, who knew the working-class well, has set
all this out very impartially and critically.[5] The condition
of the workers in capitalist society does not necessarily
get worse, as Marx requires that it shall in his *Verelendungstheorie*. The labour movement, which is an empirical
class war, has improved things for them and also made
them hopelessly bourgeois. The French socialists of the

---

[5] See his *Au delà du marxisme*.

"left" actually complain that the workers are content and do not want a revolution, and it is that, moreover, that explains the falling-off of revolutionary syndicalism in France. The same may be said of the labour-movement in England. Trade unions increase the power and social importance of the workers in contemporary society and by so doing weaken the revolutionary and anti-bourgeois spirit. Socialism is definitely becoming a party which supports good order; the practical reforming elements are coming uppermost in social-democracy and the revolutionary and messianic *pathos* is vanishing.

Communists are most indignant at this state of affairs, but they are themselves only the bourgeois of tomorrow or the day after. They can, like Marx, fight the bourgeoisie with the revolutionary spirit, but that is an unstable and passing phase, a brief moment in the conflict; things soon quiet down, the building-up of life begins again, and the bourgeois spirit reappears. This is true even of Soviet Russia where, at the heart of the communist revolution, a new bourgeoisie is unquestionably forming, a bourgeoisie crueller and more avid for life than the one that preceded it.

The positive ideals of socialists and communists are eminently middle-class: the ideals of the dreary paradise of the factory, of power, of material prosperity. This does not at all exclude the presence of a positive truth in Communism and Socialism. But it is no good fighting the bourgeois spirit with an economic system (that is a valid weapon only against Capitalism), it must be fought with another spirit: a class economic power cannot resist it, but a spiritual power can. It is in a sense true to say that all class mentality, even the proletarian, is bourgeois and shot through with a desire to exploit; the masters of tomorrow will be no less bourgeois than those of today or yesterday. The European bourgeois spirit of the nineteenth and twentieth centuries shows a great weakening of spirituality, an interest exclusively directed towards things visible, a denial of things invisible — it represents, in fact, that "economicism" so thoroughly absorbed and made absolute by Karl Marx.

Communism seems to us to be anti-bourgeois only in the degree that it is still a hidden thing, and therefore calling for faith, self-sacrifice, and enthusiasm; in so far as it has been actualized and can be seen by all it is as bourgeois as Capitalism. The bourgeois spirit is an eternal principle: Capitalism did not create it but was born of it; and Capitalism faithfully reflects the spiritual condition of contemporary society.

CHAPTER III

*The Christian Estimate of Class War • The
Christian Attitude towards Human Personality*

C HRISTIANITY MUST NOT DENY
the existence of class war under the biased pre-
text that to admit it is to imply an insufficiently
high idea of history. A realist attitude towards the social
world, to see realities without disguise, objectiveness in
matters of knowledge, have undeniably a positive moral
value from the Christian standpoint; and we are bound
to acknowledge that there is a class antagonism playing a
large part in history, that there are exploiting and exploited
classes, that class mentality perverts truth and deforms
ideas. Christian consciousness does not approve of this
aspect of the world: it regards it as most blameworthy
and a thing to be overcome.

Nevertheless, this condemnation must not be accompa-
nied by sentimental shutting of the eyes against reality or
a disdainful drawing aside from the conflict; Christians
are living in this sinful world and must bear its burden,
they may not steal away from the battlefield. Nor can the
Christian religion establish an economic system that will
be valid for everybody, everywhere, and for all time; the
Church does not profess political and economic truths, she

leaves social creation to man's freedom. But the relations between man and man are subject to her judgement and need its active criticism: and the pitiless selfishness of competition, the turning of man into a thing and of his work into a commercial commodity, are intolerable to the Christian conscience.

Now we are forced to recognize that these things are the basis of capitalist society.

Christianity has to condemn the exploitation of man by man and of class by class from a religious and moral point of view, and she has to protect the workers and the exploited, for the Christian faith attaches a value beyond price to personality and to the human soul. Therefore it is impossible for her to refrain from condemning also that regime under which this personality and this soul are turned into a means towards the unhuman economic process.

All this involves Capitalism on the one hand and Communism on the other.

Economics exist for man, and not man for economics. There is nothing more inconsistent with Christianity than the optimistic idea that the economically strongest and most successful are of necessity the best, that wealth is a favour granted to man as a reward for his virtues. Christian consciousness is the one that most easily and systematically recognizes that historical and economic categories are not eternal and that the most ephemeral of these phases is precisely that of the capitalist economy. The spiritual foundations of society are eternal, all others are temporary. The principle of private property has a certain ontological nucleus, but its forms are historical and therefore variable and passing; and it is a sin for Christians to make these forms into absolutes, all the more so since it is particularly difficult to detect the ontological nucleus in the character which private property has under our capitalist regime. The fact is that Capitalism destroys private property, it takes all meaning and justification away from it and makes it a fiction. The capital of financiers is collective and not personal, and the result is that neither the subject nor the object of property is clearly defined.

Since Christianity is concerned with realities and not with fictions it follows that the thing which is dearest to the Christian consciousness in economic life is that which is the real foundation of that life, namely, work. To Christianity work is sacred; she takes it under her protection and defends the right to property that accrues from it. The Gospel tells us that "the workman is worthy of his meat" (Matt 10:10), and St. Paul declares that "if any man will not work, neither let him eat" (2 Thess. 3:10). While the old Greco-Roman world despised work as a thing for slaves, Christianity brought about respect both for it and for those who did it. Jesus Christ, the Son of the Most High God, was in his humanity a carpenter; he belonged to the "working-class," and so did his Apostles. This fact by itself makes the social lot of the workers holy. In the Christian economy the fundamental problem is summed up in the matter of work, and the attitude taken up in regard of that determines the attitude in regard of social classes and their conflict.

Strictly speaking, there has so far been no really free work; only for artizans has it been relatively so. In the past it was always in its dominant forms a slavery or a serfdom. It is called free in capitalist society, but this shows how the use of the word freedom lends itself to equivocation, for Capitalism only substituted a new and disguised form of servile work for the one that existed before. The

working-man, that is to say, the man without means of
production, who can live only by selling his labour, is
constrained by nobody; he enjoys identical political rights
with the capitalist, he takes part in parliamentary elections:
but in reality his liberty is simply the freedom to die of
hunger if he prefers that alternative to the painful and
degrading work of a factory. Freedom of work means the
freedom to sell one's work as though it were merchandize,
and this freedom must be exercised under a threat of starvation. The buyers' conditions are made in accordance
with the unescapable position of the sellers; the buyer is
in a position to wait and choose, the seller is not.

Socialists have always aspired to set the workers and
their work free, but the striking thing is that they have
no more attempted to set out the problem of work in its
essence in their systems of ideas than have the bourgeois
themselves. They try to free the workers from hours that
are too hard or too long, but interiorly they do not hallow
work itself; this reproach is due especially to Marxism,
which takes over the forms of work established in industrial capitalist society. It would seem that this is the rock
on which socialist ideologies split, for the social question
is in the first place a matter of the organization of work
so that it shall be effectively free. Communism solves the
problem by the institution of forced labour by the state!
When all is said and done, the economic rights and interests of the working-man are not safeguarded by any social
system, for all such systems give a primacy to society over
human personality; this is true even of Capitalism, for all
its hypocritical talk about personal enterprise and private
property. The problem of work is religious and spiritual,
and the future life of society is closely bound up with its
solution. The old disciplines of work, all of them servile in

one way or another, are collapsing and it is very doubtful if they can ever be re-established, for henceforward the working classes will refuse slavery in any form, whether obvious or concealed.

And it is here that arises, in all its acuteness, the question of the religious attitude of human personality towards the work of oneself and of others, the ethics of work, a matter indissolubly bound up with a religious attitude towards life in general. Work is the basis of all social life, as well as of economics, and the social question is a Christian question precisely in that work is involved; the problem of the spiritual foundation of work is the problem of the spiritual foundation of society. Work is the heritage of man in the natural world, it is his ineluctable destiny; man as such is a workman, a toiler, and he ought to know why this is so and where the meaning of his toil is to be looked for.

It is not enough to try and get rid of the more unpleasant kinds of labour, to improve conditions and to shorten hours, which can be done by means of social activity and reforms; there is work itself, the interior attitude towards it, to be considered, and that is a question that is necessarily spiritual and religious and that cannot be answered externally. Nor can it be answered apart from Christianity, except in a servile way by enslaving the spirit to the material world. Economic life depends on work, which itself depends on spirit and is a spiritual activity energizing in a physical environment; the same can be said of manual work. So we come back to Marx's thesis.

It is nonsensical to look on work as a material phenomenon. Marx stresses his economic materialism because he was interested in only the social forms of work and did not arrive at its essence. The spirit is activity and creation

and freedom, but in the material world spiritual activity
and creation are on the wane and its freedom comes into
collision with the force of necessity. Work is not necessarily creative and the sharpest point of the labour problem
is exactly this matter of uncreative work, which is often
repellent in itself and meaningless for the person concerned.
Hard and rough economic toil, the active expression of
that anxiety for the morrow that has been bred in man
by sin, always recalls his banishment from Paradise, the
irremediable loss of the economy of Eden, the poorness and
the fewness of the material goods that are within his reach.
We may and we must want to lighten the social burden
of work; to maintain it as it is in our social system on a
plea of Christian asceticism is nothing else than a piece
of hypocrisy — and a bourgeois attitude at that.

Parallel to the social level is the individual level, but
they have no common measure. The yoke of work is the
personal destiny of man, and as such it must be borne reli-
giously; considered internally, work is an eternal ascetical
element in life. Man is forced to work by the necessity of
the material world; but because he is a free spirit he can
accept the fact as his spiritual path, as his personal *askesis*,
as a service to be given in a supra-personal cause.

The problem of labour discipline in the socialist "collectivity" is very complex and has not yet been solved. The
spiritual problem of work, its free acceptance, is aggravated
in such a society, for unless there is some internal motive
for work the workers will have to be coerced by a military
system and the world will become like a barracks. Materialistic Socialism puts its hope (I don't know quite why) in
a re-birth of human nature which will result automatically
in a new organization of society. But as the spiritual lever
has not been found this is simply a vicious circle.

Of course, the labour question is only one aspect of that social problem which, as I have said, is for Christians primarily a matter of attitude towards work, of work as a right and as a duty. There is another aspect on which the Christian verdict must be given: that of the objective final causes of economic life, of the economic plan, of organization overcoming the anarchy of the capitalist regime which is based on the interplay of individual interests and on the frenzied competition and clash of contradictory forces.

Thanks to the rationalization of industry and to the dizzying increase of commodities and economic wealth this regime produces unemployment and throws millions of men (intellectual as well as manual workers) on the street, sentencing them to misery and hunger; and it has got to go. A regime which allows of revolting indigence in spite of a general increase of wealth, which is obliged in the name of economic interest to destroy "superfluous" goods although there are people in need of them, which breeds abominable wars, which is possessed by a greed for riches which has become transformed into a disinterested passion, which empties the life even of the directing classes of meaning by making it an accessory of the economic game, such a regime is completely mad and stands condemned by conscience and by reason.

Capitalism is in principle much less coherent than Communism. It creates "enchanted money," as Carlyle caustically puts it, and is of all systems the furthest removed from realities; it is phantasmic, full of fictions, the most abnormal in the history of mankind, for more than any other it subjects the living man to impersonal arrangements. The financial world of money, banks, and the stock exchange forms a mysterious world of its own; it may even be called a mystic for, as Léon Bloy has shown so remarkably in

his *Le Salut par les Juifs*, there is an effective mysticism
of money: it is neither divine nor natural but diabolic,
and in secret it rules the world. The working classes are
not the only victims of this phantasmic world, all suffer
from it; man perishes therein and his image is obscured.
Contemporary capitalists are haunted by a frantic need for
more markets, and they themselves are falling victims to the
wild unhuman forces that they serve. They have nothing
to hold on to, they cannot stop themselves: their spirit
fails, for they can no longer contemplate divine things.

It is absolutely mistaken to suppose that the contemporary bourgeois, Capitalism's hero and the master of the
world, leads a life of inactivity and idleness: only demagogic prejudice attempts to sustain such a statement.
On the contrary, he works without intermission; he is
continually taken up with business affairs and has not a
minute's liberty. But the point is to know the quality of
his occupations, in what spirit he undertakes them, and
what use they are to his soul. Certainly no class can live
exclusively parasitically, such indolence would be perverse
and corrupt; but under Capitalism the very work of the
governing classes, the successes and failures that fill their
days, are out of accord with the Christian idea of work
and with the attitude which every Christian should have
towards life.

The capitalist regime is of all the most uncertain and
unstable; it easily leads to crises and catastrophes, nobody
knows what the morrow will bring forth, behind it lurks
an all-consuming covetousness which breeds endless dis-
quiet. The capitalist world gives happiness to nobody. Such
is its lack of fixity and assurance that the future of the
proletariat is no more secure than that of the bourgeoisie;
the millionaire, the owner of a huge business, the rich

banker, may be penniless tomorrow morning; it is a regime of risk and opportunism. It is very dynamic, expending immense energy and developing the material powers of production, but it is the ruin of men and deforms the soul alike of employers and employed.

Such is the kingdom of Mammon, and Christianity condemns it not only from the point of view of the working classes but equally from the point of view of the interests of the bourgeoisie: for these also are spiritually enslaved to a god who requires human sacrifices. Christianity calls upon us to abandon the world of shams and to return to authentic realities.

That does not mean that she decries all economic and industrial development and demands a return solely to trades and to rural economy, but she does require the establishment of a hierarchy of values and the subjection of economic life to a spiritual principle, that is, the suppression of its immoral autonomy. It is only on this condition that man can free himself from phantasms and turn again to reality.

When we speak hardly of the capitalist regime and show up its deficiencies and rank growths we do not claim, as the Marxists and communists do, thereby to have exhausted its content. Life is infinitely complex. Even the bourgeoisie is made up of people whose traits are not wholly negative and towards whom an humane attitude and appreciation are due. But at the same time the bourgeois spirit of Capitalism has branded the whole life of our age with a sinister mark; it even determines the socialists' movement itself, try as they do to disprove it.

There are absolute values, not of social origin but manifesting themselves in social life, which Christianity cannot neglect. Principal among them are the values of the human

person as the spiritual centre of life, and of freedom of
spirit, conscience, thought, and creation in work. Social systems which misunderstand or deny these stand condemned
by that fact alone. But, of course, this is not to say that,
empirically, the judgements and recognitions of Christianity in action have always been determined accordingly.
There have been theocratic social systems, papocaesarist in
the West, caesaropapist in the East, which stifled personality,
denied liberty of conscience, and misused the soul: but all
these pseudo-Christian systems were doomed to disappear
sooner or later. Historically, Russian Orthodoxy was closely
allied with the big merchants and small traders, French
Catholicism with the aristocracy, German Protestantism
with nationalism and the middle-classes. But from the point
of view of worth the human person is above the class, as
he is above the State and above economics. A person as
person does not belong to any class and is distinguished as
bourgeois, noble, peasant, or proletarian only by accidental
circumstances, by his "wrapper": he belongs by his inner
being to the spiritual world and to eternity.

Materialistic Communism and Capitalism are equally
liable to condemnation at the bar of the absolute values of
Christianity, for they have a common principle. Marxian
socialism sets class above personality and regards man solely
as a function of society, nor do the bourgeois and capitalist
ideologies see him differently; we find the same domination
by an impersonal "collective" in both Capitalism and Communism. One such collective simply prepares the ground
for another — which is just what Marx told us. Christianity
has to approach the social question with its own proper
canons of value. It appreciates a fraternal communality
and a catholicity of personalities, but it flatly refuses to
recognise the unhuman and impersonal social collective.

Man comes first in the social problem, because it is on his account that it has to be solved. Classes are fugitive, economic goods are ephemeral: the human soul is eternal, and that soul alone will stand before the throne of God. It is impossible completely to dismiss the class war when it is a matter of finding a solution of our social question; but this solution will not be found only in material and economic considerations (as the Marxists say) because the problem is also spiritual, religious, moral, educational, and technical: there has to be a spiritual renewal and education of the people at large. Unless the whole subject is gone into more deeply there is grave danger of all reform or revolution ending only in deception and pretence: the bottles would be new, but it would be the same old sour wine. Moreover, the birth of new human souls is involved, and that cannot be brought about mechanically. And there cannot be established a rule of work unless the spiritual and moral attitude towards work is radically altered.

In the ultimate analysis the social problem of this age is historiosophic: it has an eschatological element which involves a terrible judgement on our civilization and a reprobation of the old world. For Marx too it was primarily historiosophic, the coming of a new age, but he could not explain it properly because of his *naïf* materialism. This historiosophic character of Socialism has been best understood and related to an eschatology by Tillich, the German speculator on religious socialism: he renders it by the word *kairos*, the fulfilling of the times, the breaking of eternity into time.[1]

---

[1] See *Kairos, Zur Geisteslage und Geisteswerdung*. Herausgegeben von Paul Tillich.

CHAPTER IV

Real & Formal Freedom • The Man, The Citizen,
The Producer • Freedom & Coercion

THE DECLARATION OF THE RIGHTS of Man and of the Citizen [1789] cannot be said to have given much attention to "man." He was rather put in the background by "the citizen," who was understood as a political animal and his rights as formal rights. So the declaration easily degenerated into a charter of protection for bourgeois interests and the capitalist system. Furthermore, in the bourgeois liberal conception of the world rights were severed from obligations and hence expressed only interests and claims. But in reality right cannot be disassociated from duty (as in the bourgeois estimation of it, which cloaks a class greed), since one involves the other, and in a certain sense right is itself a duty.

The declaration has a very different meaning for the Christian consciousness than it has in the liberal democratic systems. In Christianity it is not the citizen but the man who enjoys absolute rights, in his capacity of a free spiritual being, and these rights cannot be separated from their corresponding duties. The very freedom of a man is not a claim but an obligation, it gives less than it demands. God requires that man shall be free; he must take up the burden of freedom as a young man takes up privileges and responsibilities when he comes of age. The centre of gravity is not with the citizen but with the man. The notion of citizenship is secondary and subordinate, belonging to that political society wherein realities are so well disguised that it is difficult to see them. The notion of man, on the contrary, belongs to the spiritual world wherein his absolute and indefeasible rights are rooted. But the declaration of rights cannot limit itself to the proclamation of the rights of man as a spiritual creature, it must also touch the inferior and subordinate levels of being.

This is how the reality of spiritual life was superseded by the reality of economic life.

In this sphere the declaration became related to the rights of the producer and worker, a notion which belongs to economic, not to political society, but it is unquestionably the sphere of important and serious realities, on which the life of man depends at the material level. Saint-Simon, and after him Proudhon, in a different way, both proposed to substitute the rights of the producer for the rights of man; this suggestion follows from a view of society which sees it primarily as working, and in fact the producer is a more real being than the citizen. Thus we pass into the actual domain of work, considered in all its hierarchical degrees, and that is how socialists generally refuse to consider it.

But a declaration of the economic rights of the producer disassociated from the spiritual rights of man enslaves the human being to the material world and leads to a qualitative lowering of the level of culture. From the standpoint of worth, the hierarchy of degrees and values is, first of all, the according of primacy to spirit; then, economic considerations; and lastly, politics as the instrument of economics. Politics can be prevented from degenerating into a fiction that hides the game of commercial interests only by being consciously subject to economics, which in their turn are subordinate to the spiritual principle. Society must be conceived as working and creating, based on spiritual and economic foundations and conceding only the necessary minimum of influence to politics. Self-sufficient political vampirism exhausts human societies and builds a fictitious structure which, so far from serving life and vital interests, subjects them to its own. Hence it is that a self-denying ordinance in respect of politics is needful and an emergence of real spheres of spiritual and economic life indispensable.

There is what determines our attitude towards social classes. We cannot count on the social results to be obtained by civil and political equality as it was established in the bourgeois democracies after the suppression of social ranks, because the disproportion between the formal and the real in it is too flagrant. In spite of contemporary democratic equality the economic class inequalities that permeate the whole of life are very great indeed.

That simply proves how much more real and primeval economics are than politics.

The Declaration of Rights has not been deepened in democratic societies to the point where real economic rights can be insisted on. The right in property is recognized and guaranteed, but it is that of those in possession and not the right in or to property of the poor man and the "worker." Society does not recognize the most real of all rights, the right to life, for, since so monstrous a phenomenon as unemployment can belong to wealthy societies, it cannot be admitted that there is any recognized right to work. And what is the acknowledged formal liberty of all citizens worth? — it means this, that many are in fear for tomorrow, that many are hungry and in want, while others enjoy colossal fortunes. The existing disproportion between formal liberty and real liberty is due to the fact that in the economic world liberty is not determined formally but materially, by the means and methods of production. The sentimental and rhetorical defence of liberty in which bourgeois orators indulge when they are attacking the iniquities of Socialism shows how that grand word can be abused and what varied meanings are given to it.

I often call to mind a well-known anecdote, attributed, if I am not mistaken, to Louis Blanc.[1] A well-to-do man was walking past a cab and he said to the driver, "Are you free?" (i.e., disengaged). "Free," was the reply. "Long live freedom!" exclaimed the passer-by and went on his road. Truly, such an interpretation of the words freedom and liberty is quite permissible, and it is the one most favoured in capitalist society. But we must combat it with a real conception of liberty in social life, a freedom that will enable man not only to gain his livelihood but also to use his creative powers and follow his true calling: in a word, real freedom requires that the organization of society be such as will guarantee the opportunity of work and of creation to every man. This implies the disappearance of both social ranks and classes and their replacement by the trades and professions; and a society based on work organized in its hierarchical degrees, that is, on real life, inevitably must produce a new type of corporate organization that would form as it were the primary cells of the body politic. All this implies a notion of work diametrically opposed to

---

[1] Louis Blanc (1811–1882) was a French socialist politician, journalist and historian. — Ed.

that of Marxism and materialistic Socialism, which look
to quantity at the expense of quality.

A mechanical equality is entirely foreign to Christianity,
because it is out of harmony with the nature of human
being and tends to its destruction, and the doing away with
ranks and classes does not mean the production of such
an artificial uniformity and levelling-down, the negation
of qualitative hierarchy. Quite the reverse: it means the
restoration of a true human hierarchy in opposition to
the conventional and symbolical subordination resulting
from the class system. And so it would become possible to
form authentically ontological estimates of man, measuring
him by what he is and not by what he has.

The human body must be seen naked in order to know
its beauty, and in the same way Christianity demands that
realities shall be stripped of their artificial adornments.
Only a society of trades and professions and creative voca-
tions which has rejected the rank and class system can be
free from fictions and shams. But it does not end there.
It must be a society wherein the sinful desire for power,
which breeds vampirism, crass delusions, and the swindle
of politics, shall have been reduced as far as possible. All
hierarchy of quality will not be absent from this new
society which man is so painfully seeking, but the aristocracy of birth and fortune will give place to an aristocracy
of quality in work and creation, ability and calling, an
effectively human aristocracy. In such a society freedom
and love would be one.

Class antagonism and warfare has polluted the human
soul with the poisons of covetousness, enmity, and hatred,
and the souls of the proletarians have suffered and suc-
cumbed as much as those of the bourgeois. This psychological and moral fact is sufficient by itself to bring down the

condemnation of Christianity upon class society and the existence of classes. It may be objected, of course, that hate, animosity, and envy are indestructible and that they will be found in every society so long as sin has not been finally defeated. This is true, but in my opinion this truth does not exclude the possibility, nay, the necessity, of enquiring what social regime is likely to bring the most equitable and least prejudicial results to human souls. Class hatred is so widespread that one sometimes loses all hope of a peaceful settlement: it seems as if all negotiations have failed and that it is already too late; too much explosive matter has been stored up, too much integrality and unity lost; surely the idea of co-operation and solidarity between classes is a sentimental dream. Marx did not foresee everything and many things have not happened in the way he prophesied, but the implacable class hatred that tears contemporary society apart unhappily confirms much that he foretold. Though we, as Christians, part company with Marx in his estimates of value, it is most certainly not in order that we may side with and support the cause of capitalism and the bourgeoisie. All class mentality smothers the spiritual man and paralyzes the Christian conscience, whether of noble, bourgeois, or proletarian; all such mentality is equally unlawful to a Christian and he is bound in morals to condemn it.

Socially speaking, the proletariat is right to fight the bourgeoisie, but its mentality is so poisoned with resentment and anger and breathes such a sombre jealousy of the cultured people that its spirit is seen to be far from that of a messiah who shall set mankind free; rather does it display hardship and humiliation seeking their revenge. Herbert Spencer once said that you cannot expect golden conduct from leaden instincts, and that is an indisputable elementary truth. The proletarian, in the Marxist sense, is necessarily bitter, envious, vindictive, and prone to violence. That is exactly what the communists want him to be, and their demagogy is directed towards the production of just such a state of soul. But how can it be expected that these "leaden instincts" will one day lead to a new and better social system, to new and better relations between men? The "proletarian" thus understood must not be identified with the worker, for the last can have quite other instincts and states of soul; he can be a Christian and look for a social regime that will be more human and more just.

Man's hatred for man and for a whole class of men is sinful and deserving of blame, but we must not forget that this hatred was the psychological effect of the arrogance and contempt which the governing classes, noble and bourgeois, showed for the working people. Payment of the debt due for slavery and serfdom is now being demanded, and the old sin breeds a new one. Clearly the most blameworthy is he who first took up this wicked attitude towards his fellow-men.

The social phenomenon of spiteful jealousy now manifests itself as much against culture, education, and knowledge as against personal wealth. This is beyond doubt sinful, and the society in which this phenomenon has arisen is condemned to death. Moral consciousness joins with that of the socialists in being unable longer to put up with the forms of social and economic inequality which have been suffered hitherto. Even the members of the privileged classes who enjoy such great riches by contrast with the penury and destitution of so many others are beginning to feel uncomfortable and to have doubts of the security and justice of a regime which has given them a monopoly of good things. It is unquestionable that all classes want, though as yet in a confused sort of way, a solution of the social question, and some in the directing classes are showing sympathy for the theories of Tolstoi (rather than those of Marx).

At the same time it cannot be denied that bourgeois self-affirmation still has the ascendancy in world politics; the change in feeling and consciousness just referred to is valuable chiefly as a symptom indicative of the crisis through which contemporary society is passing. Bourgeois morality and ideas are reaching a more and more advanced stage of decadence, and the younger generations have no use for either. Men naturally continue to follow their instincts and defend their own interests, but unhappily or cynically, no longer believing in the validity of their principles. There are many indications that this settled form of society and civilization is dying, and that a period of change has begun which will last for a long time.

Betterment of the economic conditions of the working class is not sufficient to settle the social problem. Capitalism has got to go entirely. But it is primarily a psychological and moral question. Socialism will probably aggravate the situation, though it seems to me that in so far as it is not materialist it will help to clear the moral atmosphere and make the relations between men more brotherly and human. The bourgeois mentality and consciousness, due like those of the proletariat to the loss of Christianity and decay of spirituality, are inconsistent with Christianity, whatever those pseudo-Christians who have adapted themselves to bourgeois requirements may say. The period of the first money-cult in England must horrify any man with a shred of Christian conscience. But neither shall we find a new man in the proletarian who wants to be lord of the earth; when he is thoroughly examined and his

halo pulled off he is found to be the same old bourgeois
nicely got up in a new dress: it is the old Adam become
his own slave. Moral beauty, like physical beauty, abides
in only a few of the dwellers on this earth. Even the communistic atheism of the proletariat is purely bourgeois, an
inheritance from the "Age of Enlightenment."

Christianity does not accept the sufficiency of class
and its hatreds, the denial by one class of the image and
likeness of God in the representatives of another class. We
may violently repudiate the bourgeois spirit and principles,
we may fight against a social system — but we may not
hate the bourgeois as a human being with all his varied
attributes. Moreover, there is a psychological law by virtue
of which he who hates comes to resemble the person hated.

All the same, it would be hypocritical from a Christian
point of view to reject all forms of class war and to avoid
them as though unclean. Under Capitalism the subdued
and exploited workers must strive for the improvement
of their social condition, not only in their own subjective
interest but for the sake of an objective truth. The worker
is not fighting for himself alone but for the whole body
of working-men; the end in view is a universal human
justice: it is a campaign of a class against the power of
money. Bourgeois liberalism wanted to give the worker
all the formal rights due to an atom, make him equal to
every other atom, and then keep him isolated. Isolated
working-men are powerless to improve their situation or to
do anything else; an organized union is their only strength
and hope. This can be seen particularly well in England,
where the trade-unions practically direct the political life
of the country. At the present time, generally speaking,
the right of the workers to organize themselves is recognized, and this means a certain limitation of contemporary

individualism and "atomism"; but the most innocent of such associations constitutes a form of class war against the capitalists.

The Holy See, which officially recognizes professional groups and encourages the formation of unions of Catholic working-men, condemns class war.[2] There would seem to be a clear contradiction here, for class war does not necessarily mean violence and bloody revolutions; its manifestations may be quite peaceable. To deny the right to strike on the ground of absolute moral principles is unjust; it implies inability to see effective abuses (cloaked under appeals to law and order) which are often infinitely greater than those arising from strikes.[3]

A normal social and economic life is inconceivable as the collision and reciprocal action of isolated atoms; it can come about only by a principle of co-operation. Capitalism has long since ceased to be individualistic and become collectivist; its great trusts have no relation to individualist economies. Formerly it saw the guarantee of the freedom of personality in preventing the workers from being in a position to carry on a class war, and it resigned itself to making concessions in favour of the movement for the defence of the workers' interests very unwillingly. The result is that the real force limiting the power of capital for the good of bourgeois society is not the efforts of socialist parliamentary parties but the activities of the trade-unions, and society is moving little by little towards a new type of syndicalist regime. Marx, who lived in times very different from our own and did not suspect the subsequent

---

[2] See the encyclical *Quadragesimo anno* of Pope Pius XI on the social question (and that of Leo XIII, *Rerum Novarum*). [TR.]

[3] This is a misunderstanding of Catholic teaching. The right to strike in certain circumstances is expressly recognized. [TR.]

developments either of capital or of labour, put no faith in such a regime; De Man puts syndicalism and Marxism in opposition very soundly. The fact is that in Soviet Russia there is no workers' class war; Communism has taken the form of State Capitalism and allows no professional and trade associations which do not depend directly on itself. After having absorbed personality, society in turn finds itself absorbed by the state, which is thus enabled to become an oppressor and exploiter, to invent new sorts of slave labour, to turn working-men once again into bond-men, and to perfect a new system of tyranny.

Personality has been subjected to oppression through-out history, sometimes by society, sometimes by the state. Lorenz von Stein, who was one of the first to establish a decisive distinction between society and the state and who detected the existence of class war, believed that society has a natural tendency to produce inequality and that the emergence of the castes marked its victory over the state, which had up till then been the persecutor of personali-ty.[4] Thus he is inclined to see the state as the defender of "labour" and the working-man, and to put it above "class," but he does not end by identifying it with society, as Com-munism does. In the communist system the supreme centre, the depository of reason and the fount of consciousness, is the "collective," which is supra-social as well as supra-personal; it is not the interest of the workers that matters but the might and the development of the collective for the glorification of the communist state. This is the result of the *pathos* of power with which Marxism is imbued.

To this idea must be opposed a campaign on behalf of a certain dignity in life, of the right to work and to enjoy

---

[4] See his *Geschichte der sozialen Bewegung in Frankreich.*

the property accruing from one's work, of the rights of the consumer as well as of the producer. The consequences of the rationalization of industry, particularly as seen in the United States, show that actually the social problem is much more a question of distribution and of consumption than of production. It is also clearly a matter of technique, whose bewildering achievements (unforeseen by Marx) are precisely what have made the Marxian theory of class war ineffective for today. But technique and "rationalization" alone cannot solve the problem, for they leave its essential point, the relations between man and man, untouched; they are more useless than anything else, because it is technical progress itself that so aggravates the moral and spiritual sides of the difficulty.

It would be atrociously dishonest and wrong to wait for social improvement to follow man's moral perfecting; we must work actively for the reform of society. But every time that anybody begins to do so, whether by the protection of women and children in industry or by the reduction of hours or hardship in the working-day or by bringing about a more equitable incidence of taxation, the representatives of the directing classes protest against what they call an infringement of liberty. Now there is a social reality of a particular kind actually in existence, and it requires from us active interest and participation; we are bound to take part in it, to vote for this or that; we may no longer shelter behind the wall of neutrality. It is our duty to feed the hungry socially as well as individually. We must not forget that by refusing the troubles attendant on a change in the social order we choose to accept the abuses inherent in a maintenance of the present state of things. The capitalist regime is itself a kind of camouflaged violation, and it is a mistake, wilful or innocent, to believe that those who defend the *status quo* are not by that fact using violence and that only those who fight Capitalism are guilty of criminal subversion. In capitalist society property is equivalent to a coercion and disinheriting of men, and consequently we are not free to affirm that its limitation, whether by society or by the state, in favour of property acquired by work is an outrage or that its protection is legitimate.

It is very necessary to examine the correlation of freedom and force, liberty and violence, for they are often responsible for mistakes and misunderstandings. Apparent freedom may well conceal a real compulsion and, inversely, apparent compulsion may be really a setting-free. Defence of freedom, that is, of the ultimate value, can easily be turned into a mere conservative principle which upholds the existing abuses of power to which we are accustomed; freedom is often understood and defended in such a way that all change or progress is impossible. A man in a materially privileged position is prone to see an arbitrary violation of his liberty in every reform which alters and improves the social regime; especially does he view a reduction of his income in this way. During a revolution, it is not only the fact of being imprisoned, of being refused freedom of speech, of being shot, that appears to him as criminal violence, but also the deprivation of those legal and economic advantages that were formerly his due. On the other hand, a man who is materially poor and degraded welcomes the reorganization of society as a deliverance, and sees criminal violence in the maintenance of a regime in which he was destitute and unhappy.

There is a sense in which every displacement is an exercise of force on the material world. When I get up to go into another room and speak to somebody I bring about a whole series of coercive changes in the world about me: I push back my chair, I open the door, I make the person in the next room turn round and listen to me. So long as I stop where I am, my surroundings seem to be free and unconstrained. Freedom is sometimes understood to be summed up in the exclamation "O, go to hell!"

The complexity of the problem of freedom and force in social reality, particularly in its material aspect, can be judged from even so simple an illustration. When man has experienced a long state of slavery he comes to look on it as normal and unalterable, even as freedom, and there must be a change in his consciousness before it appears to him as an intolerable wrong. Everything is so warped in capitalist society that the understanding of independence and constraint has been completely falsified: a change in what is usual is by many called "using force," just measures taken by society and the state to draw on personal superfluity of wealth are hailed as outrages; it is the same when pressure of circumstances makes those people do some work. They never stop to consider that these "constraints" may be perfectly equitable and liberating as affecting those whose burden of life has been too heavy. The bourgeois cannot justly complain of being subjected to violence short of being shot or put in prison or having their movements restrained.

When a man is deprived of elementary economic rights and has no control over the means of production he is forced to sell his labour as a commodity; that is coercion, and a regime which allows that state of things is based on despotism. If the workman is ill-used, if he has to put up with bad conditions on pain of losing his job and consequently his livelihood, though his work may be called free because he can leave it at will, nevertheless there

is frightful pressure put upon him and his liberty is an
illusion. If a man is accorded the right freely to hold his
convictions and beliefs but at the same time his material
well-being depends on individuals who require of him
other convictions and beliefs, there again is coercion and a
suppression of freedom enforced by fear of starvation. The
domination of public opinion sometimes involves terrible
violation of the personal conscience, and even degenerates
into a complete tyranny. In contemporary society "free-
thinkers" subject Christians to a persecution of this kind.

In studying the reformation of society from a Christian
point of view the problem of freedom and force is found
to be so complex that it requires very deep thought and
a most acute perception for its examination. Christianity
can in no wise subscribe to the forms of violence and
compulsion exercised by the Russian communists, who use
murder, terrorism, and the deprivation of the elementary
liberties of man, of his conscience and of his mind, as
permissible means for the creation of a new society. Nevertheless, the Christian conscience may and must sanction
certain kinds of social pressure, which must be looked
on as instruments for the service of one's neighbour, for
without them not only real freedom but also the material
support of unfortunate men are impossible. Real liberty
implies in physical life an economic guarantee for all; it
supposes a social regime in which no man is required to
make a living at the price of over-arduous or degrading
work or of the integrity of his conscience.

That is why we must not repudiate a class war. The
point is that it must be spiritualized: it must be kept in
subordination to the supreme spiritual principle and away
from the control of revengeful passions and relentless
violence.

CHAPTER V

The Aristocrat, The Bourgeois, & The Workman

A CCORDING TO MARX, SOCIAL
classes are determined simply and solely by reference to economics and economic production,
and in consequence he does not go into and explain their
different psychic types. As a matter of fact his psychology
is always very crude; he does not characterize so much
as judge. But the respective characteristics of aristocracy,
bourgeois, and working-class are of very great interest from
the point of view of social psychology, for they represent
different spiritual breeds as well as different social types. If
Marx had not been obsessed by the idea that economics are
the determining cause of every reality, he would have seen
that there is an infinitely greater difference between the
aristocrat and the bourgeois than between the bourgeois
and the worker; the first two belong to different breeds,
the second pair to one and the same, differentiated only
by a family quarrel. The aristocratic type and the working
type represent independent values; the bourgeois, in spite
of current opinion, does not.

The patrician type is not determined by temporary
economic conditions; they are only a secondary factor in
it. An aristocracy may be very wealthy, and has been so

in the past, but its material resources do not originate in economic enterprise and initiative; they were acquired by the sword and then became hereditary; and it is lacking in all economic virtues, which are indeed specifically bourgeois. Aristocracy resides primarily in nobility of descent, in its conservation and elaboration, in the hereditary transmission of "blue blood"; its status is not conditioned by economics, but depends first of all on birth and the good qualities of ancestors. An aristocrat may be totally ruined and his family in the course of generations deteriorate and lose its social position, as happened in Russia to certain princely houses of the line of Rurik; but this phenomenon is of secondary importance, for the nobility of the family remains despite the loss of all material resources. The bourgeois who in the same circumstances has to work in some humble capacity to earn his daily bread thereby loses everything, there is nothing left to show his former social position. The aristocrat working in a factory is still an aristocrat: his hands, his face, his manner, his voice, all betray his origin; centuries have gone to his fashioning and his characteristics have been handed on from generation to generation.

The economic privileges of the patrician have not been gained by his personal efforts, as have those of the bourgeois. Without doubt his ancestors were given to armed pillage, in accordance with the general practice of the past, but he is the last man who can be reproached with the velleities of money; he is incapable, so to say, of "being successful" and making himself rich, rather is he much more inclined to waste his fortune. He carries about with him the memory of the bravery of his ancestors and is unmindful of their cruelties and wrong-doing; everything he has, his estates and his spiritual endowments, is derived from them, he is the result of a long and slow process of growth. And the longer it has subsisted the more authentic an aristocracy is. It has profited by its possibilities of leisure, without which it would not have formed the high type of culture and refinement of living which other classes have tried to imitate; its courtesy and "good breeding" have a cultural value of universal importance. It is essentially generic, and therein lie both its strength and its weakness. The aristocrat is the opposite of the bourgeois in everything: the one remembers the past and treasures the stories of bygone generations; the other is indifferent to the past, except sometimes to its more recent years, and lives only in the present. Distinguished bourgeois families can often show a long descent and are proud of it, but they represent a special sort of aristocracy within the bourgeoisie. The true bourgeois is always primarily a *parvenu*, and that is *his* strength and weakness.

A whole series of special psychical characteristics accrue to the ideal aristocrat from the fact that everything he has is gratuitous, hereditary, not the result of his own efforts and work. Resentment, "touchiness," envy are foreign to him; he may give offence, he often does, but he does not readily take it: offensiveness and enviousness are not aristocratic feelings, he regards an insult as an indignity offered to the honour of himself and his ancestors and he is quick to wipe it out with blood. The value of the patrician type resides in its being a gift; it is like that physical beauty which is a grace and cannot be earned; when a man is comely by birth and breeding he need be envious of nobody on that head. The fact that the aristocrat is chiefly determined biologically and psychically and not economically is confirmed by experience; the bolshevists do not confine their attack to economic privilege, but extend it to nobility of origin, honourable ancestry, "blue blood." Nobility of birth provokes their resentment even when the man in question is, on account of the economic situation, actually a proletarian.

Aristocratism is a product of plentifulness, and material generosity and magnanimity are inherent in its true type. The aristocrat does not want to be a business-man, to amass money by work is not his line. If he tries to get richer and orders his life by economic calculations, that shows that he has let himself be "embourgeoised." Aristocratism takes for granted that I have owned something from the beginning, not that I began without something; it is *a priori*, not *a posteriori*. The typical patrician sums up the noble traits elaborated by the knighthood in an earlier stage of European society, and these characteristics of chivalry persist after that historical chivalry has gone, forming an eternal element in mankind.

The aristocracy is a particular anthropological species as opposed to the bourgeoisie. It affirms the principle of inequality. One can become bourgeois, but one must be born an aristocrat, for there is no possibility of becoming such. The "new rich" are a type in perfect conformity with the bourgeois spirit, while the newly "ennobled," who try so hard to cover up the traces of their past, always make us rather suspicious and uncomfortable; it takes a long time to make an aristocracy, but a bourgeoisie can be formed within a generation. A true aristocracy is a race of conquerors and masters, apart from the rest of society and having a different origin from other men; it has the *pathos* of remoteness and surrounds itself with a ring-fence for the avoidance of indiscriminate contact with the masses; it fears defilement by intermixture so much that it has elaborated a whole code of conventions for the defence of the exclusiveness of its life. There follows a severance from nature and the appearance of a qualitative selection of the type. An aristocracy lives isolated in its own world. Alfred de Vigny[1] justly remarks that aristocracy is based on pride, and democracy on envy, and in fact pride does seem to be the original sin of aristocracy, not a personal sin but generic and hereditary. To overcome this sin, which often has a pagan element, and to convert an aristocrat to Christianity is particularly difficult because pride begets contempt of the other classes, those commoners of undistinguished lineage. The isolation of an aristocracy, its exclusive bond with the past, its fear of "mixing," its insufficient interest in the vital things that are happening in the world, its respect for convention, all these inevitably tend to exhaustion and degeneration. It is the fate of all aristocracy, in the social sense of the word, to get soft, to give itself up entirely to amusement, gradually to lose all spirituality. Then it is marked for death. It can keep up its prestige and hegemony for a longer or shorter time, but it cannot for long stand up against the mighty forces of life and against fusion with other classes. A minority show ability to assimilate and adapt themselves to new social conditions, but the majority are incapable of it, they become embittered and decay. The members of an aristocracy who are best conserved morally are branded with an incurable weariness and appear to have lost all semblance of life.

Nevertheless, an aristocratic element forms a part of every new social regime, keeping a psychological and æsthetic value even though it has lost all social importance.

---

[1] Alfred de Vigny (1797–1863) was a French poet, early French Romanticist, and translator of Shakespeare. — Ed.

This has been the case with titled and noble families in the democratic republics of France and the Americas, where they receive almost greater respect than they did in imperial Russia. Socially speaking, aristocracy is bound to perish and cannot revive, but psychologically it will subsist because of the eternal element in it. When it has lost all social privileges and material wealth we can better appreciate the continuance of its psychical properties; not its pride and aloofness, but its refinement, its nobility, its wide-spiritedness, its freedom from resentment and pettiness. Its historical sin consists in its having made concessions to the middle-classes, adapting itself to their growing power, and in failing to support the cause of the working classes. There have been, of course, exceptions, notably in England, where the conservative party associated with the aristocracy has been inclined to ally itself more with the labour party than with the middle-class liberals; this has helped on the passing of a number of measures of social reform.[2] There is an analogous state of affairs in Germany. An aristocratic type of Socialism, hostile to bourgeois liberalism and radicalism, is perfectly possible, but, socially speaking, it cannot save the aristocracy; its social mission is at an end and it is powerless against industrialization and the feverish successes of its technique. The future belongs to a spiritual and intellectual aristocracy, which is a separate and special phenomenon.

This aristocracy is a social and psychological group which it is definitely impossible to determine according to Marxist categories. It is outside the class war, which it

---

[2] Here an Englishman may be allowed a footnote of incredulity. M. Berdyaev's bald statement is too simplistic; it does not seem to take into account the effects of political manœuvring or the nature of so much of our "aristocracy." [TR.]

will have nothing to do with, and it is committed to no other party than its own. Its representatives may sometimes associate themselves with bourgeois systems of ideas, but its fundamental interests are not economic; they are intellectual and creative, concerned with spiritual rather than material values. Accordingly, it is recruited from all classes, from the nobility and gentry, from the middle classes, from the peasants and industrial workers. In the Middle Ages this *élite* was principally concentrated in the religious houses, and the *intelligentzia* was monastic; the philosophers, scholars, artists, and writers were monks, for only in a monastery could one escape from the roughness and constant warfare of feudal life. In modern times all that is changed and the cultural importance of the ecclesiastical order is at best weakened, and at worst negligible: intellectually, the clergy have become stiff and narrow.

Spiritual and intellectual aristocracy is not inherited or generic, it is personal; its value depends on the quality, capability, and power of creation proper to an individual, it is real and not symbolical. The qualities of this class are not exclusively gratuitous or exclusively earned, but partake of the nature of both kinds. If social aristocracy gets its worth freely by inheritance, spiritual aristocracy receives it from God. The creative gifts of God, talents and genius, are not merited but free, and they are given not to be wrapped in a napkin and hidden in the earth, but to be used and developed and made fruitful; that signifies that the products of work must be added to the original gift. The prophets, the doctors of the Church, the religious and social reformers, philosophers, scholars, inventors, poets, painters, musicians, all these belong to the spiritual aristocracy and it is not possible to fit them into any scheme of classes based on economic considerations. Their life is entirely devoted to creative work of one sort or another, but this is not productive in the material and economic sense; what they do or make is appreciated often only by a very tiny minority. The members of this aristocracy, ill equipped to deal with economic matters, often find themselves in a most unenviable material position and suffer great hardships (the factory worker has far more powerful means of defence). They have been derided and persecuted first by the social aristocracy and then by the bourgeoisie, and now they run a serious risk of suffering at the hands of the proletariat.

The spiritual aristocracy cannot be assimilated to the bourgeoisie on either a psychological or social basis. The Russian communists incorporate all writers, scholars, and so on in the bourgeoisie under the vague label of *intelligentzia*; this is partly through ignorance and partly a demagogic move to flatter the bad instincts of the workers; actually, what I call the spiritual and intellectual aristocracy does not at all correspond with what a Russian understands by *intelligentzia*. It is stupid to cry up the bourgeoisie because it has produced a considerable number of men of genius, scholars, philosophers, poets, inventors, reformers, but it is no less stupid to repudiate these great men simply because they come from the bourgeois classes. The social origin of a great man has nothing to do with his genius, as the Marxists themselves recognize when it is a question of Marx or Lenin, neither of whom could boast of proletarian descent. It is of no more interest to know that Kant and Hegel and Goethe and Schiller were by birth bourgeois, than to know that Pushkin and Tolstoi belonged to the nobility. It takes a Marxist and an economic materialist to build up an *apologia* for the bourgeoisie out of the number of creative geniuses it is alleged to have begotten. Genius is not the offspring of any class, it is created by God; this is true even of the genius of those who, like Marx, turn against God.

The thing of fundamental interest is that, throughout the history of mankind, only a limited number of men have lived by spiritual and intellectual interests, devoting themselves to contemplation and creation as to autonomous values, that only a very, very few have created new values in their search after the meaning and transfiguration of life. Men can be primarily divided into those who are capable of creating and those who are not. By his nature, that work of God, every man is so capable, even if only in the form of a creative relationship with another person. But an overwhelming majority in all classes has been content to let its creative power be smothered and lives only for the worldly, economic, commercial interests of daily life, without looking for another world and a better life. If you listen to the talk of ordinary men and women, in the streets and public places or in their homes, you are horrified by the mediocrity around which their interests revolve, by their apparent incapacity to rise above a hideous commonplaceness. Every class is immersed in social "everyday life" and is tied up in its trifling laws and observances. The people at large can rise above themselves spiritually only by means of a religious life; religion is their sole spiritual food — and even that ends by coming down to their level. In a word, there is only a small minority capable of being really interested by the things of the spirit.

That is the fundamental rift in mankind, a rift infinitely deeper than any division into classes.

The aristocracy, the bourgeoisie, and the working class are now united in being orientated solely towards the world of sense, and in that respect differ only in manners

and customs, speech, style, and the things which belong
to them. The aristocracy could never be forgiven for being
capable of creative work, of living by superior interests,
spiritual and intellectual; they were looked upon as an alien
race. All the classes, generally speaking, agree in hostility
towards the spiritual and intellectual aristocracy, which
they expect to serve their interests and which they persecute if it opposes them. But there is a difficulty and a
contradiction here, for this aristocracy has itself a tendency
to deteriorate and to wear out; it becomes self-centred and
ineffective. Exceptional spiritual and intellectual gifts are
given to man for him to use creatively for the accomplish-
ment of the mission which is entrusted to him. When he
has received the gifts of God, the creative genius must give
heed to the interior voice which calls on him to serve God
and the divine image in man: not to serve average society
or class interests, but goodness, truth, and beauty. Now
a spiritual aristocracy can become deaf to this voice and
begin to serve itself in a proud isolation like that of the
social aristocracy; it can cut itself off from general society
and form an exclusive *élite*, contemptuous of the world
around it and delighting in its own superiority. To do
this is to betray its calling and enter on the road of decadence and death. But what is even worse is that this very
decadence and death may be mistaken for indications of a
superior state, such is the pride of the isolated and useless!

Spiritual aristocracy has a prophetical mission to fulfil,
in the wide sense of the word prophetical, namely, to help
on a better future, to sustain the spirit of a new life, to create new values. This spirit breathes in philosophers, poets,
artists, reformers, inventors, as well as in more strictly
religious prophets, and when it begins to decay and the
consciousness of a high calling to weaken then aristocracy

degenerates and loses its justification. When [Thomas] Carlyle speaks, in *Past and Present,* of a new aristocracy of work he obviously means an aristocracy of the prophetical ministry and of the transfiguration of life, not a vain *élite* made up of isolated aesthetes who are for ever consumers and never producers. The spirit of death which hovers over the intellectual *élite* of Europe testifies to the social crisis which is convulsing the culture of society today. But spiritual and intellectual aristocracy is an eternal element in human society without which it cannot live as it ought, it is an hierarchical principle standing upright amid the class war. And as in every authentic hierarchy each degree depends on and is joined to the one above, so the work of the technician relies on the work of the philosophers and other scientists, however little he may be aware of it.

The notion of "bourgeoisism," like that of aristocratism, can be interpreted in two ways, socially and spiritually; but, while the expression "spiritual aristocratism" corresponds to a positive increase of worth, "spiritual bourgeoisism" is a negative qualification, for the bourgeoisie is the class which is most determined by reference to economics: *homo economicus* is precisely the bourgeois man. Economics is the substantial possession and own creation of the bourgeois who, without knowing anything about Marx, is an economic materialist. His attitude to economics is quite different from that of the aristocrat, who is not interested in enriching himself and for whom the categories of economic development do not exist. The bourgeois, on the contrary, is a man who is out to get rich by his own personal efforts, initiative, and energy; economically speaking, he emerges from the depths to scale the heights. It was he who discovered evolution. Infinite expansion is natural to him. To the aristocrat it is "origins" that matter;

to the bourgeois it is "results." The one can rise no higher, he can either sink or maintain his original level; the other "gets on," makes his way, boasts that he is a self-made man. Both of them have conquered the world. But whereas in the past the man-at-arms has done it with sword and spear, in the present the business-man has done it by economic, industrial, and financial operations.

The bourgeois is a hard-working man; he does not know the leisure which the aristocrat has turned to his own advantage, he does not live for himself but for his business; even if he be a millionaire he is no less preoccupied by it, and knows nothing of aristocratic freedom from care (the only sort, by the way, that history records). The bourgeois never stops, and frequently becomes the victim of his own activity; if he lives in luxury, it is the better to meet the requirements of his work. It never occurs to the aristocrat that his material prosperity might depend on his own cleverness, presence of mind, enterprise, and skill, while the bourgeois never forgets that it actually does. A bourgeois who leads a parasitic existence and "enjoys life" is degenerate and he stands apart among his fellows; in the classical bourgeois type there is an ascetical element: he does not work for himself, but to increase and multiply economic commodities and values.[3] From him came the initiative for the development of man's economic powers, and that precisely was his mission to the world. He was gripped by a devastating passion for the discovery of new worlds, for expansion and development without limit,

---

[3] Max Weber speaks of the *innerweltliche* Askese characteristic of the founders of Capitalism, and traces it to a religious source in Calvinism. (A similar idea has been worked out in English by R. H. Tawney, Professor George O'Brien, E. S. P. Haynes, and others. Cf., also the recently published life of Rockefeller by John T. Flynn, significantly entitled *God's Gold*. [TR.])

and thereafter he became dynamic, living no longer in a stable and static cosmic order. Economic life is his sphere *par excellence*, and there he demands incessant change; he cannot bear inertia and stagnation. Robinson Crusoe is an example of this type of bourgeois in his first and best period.

There are several "layers" in the bourgeois class, each with its special psychological traits. There is on the one hand an old and dignified bourgeoisie, going back to the beginning of modern times and observant of its traditions; it is virtuous in its own way, marked with the character-istics of a particular aristocracy, hard-working in the old sense of the word, content with reasonable wealth. On the other hand there is the new bourgeoisie, which has no use for traditions and whose life is a continually feverish enterprise; it is for ever seeking profits and new ways of getting rich, and its uncontrollable impulse towards further and further economic development has given birth to the fictitious and chimerical world of contemporary Capital-ism. This new bourgeoisie, given over to self-indulgence and unrestrained luxury, has introduced an element of decomposition and decadence which already prevents further creativeness. Its interior call to action, boldness, and strength may be heard, but is no longer effective, for ideologically the new bourgeoisie cannot avoid downfall, it has lost interest in ideas, its mission seems to be ended.

The fundamental question for us is, what is the attitude of the bourgeois towards the worker?

The value of a workman corresponds to that of his work, and work is holy. The working man seems to be the nearest of all to the biblical doom on our sinful world: "In the sweat of thy face shalt thou eat bread." He carries the load of our existence, in him is concentrated that "solicitude for the world" which Heidegger regards as the essence of being. He knows only the rudiments of life and is cut off from its development, for him more than for anyone else the span of man's years is passed in a world of misery and sin, conditioned by hard necessity. Those men who are able to reach the freer spaces of being and have leisure for plentiful creation therein are few enough in number, nor is it vouchsafed to us to know why some should be thus favoured, while the many are careworn and weary with incessant toil. That is a thing that we shall understand only when we have transcended the limits of life on earth. But we do know that there is bound to be inequality and a qualitative selection from the fact that the general run of mankind is quite incapable in any circumstances of reaching a common level of free and abundant life. It was the aristocrat who by violence first established social inequality, he was the first to free himself from work and economic worry, far back in the mists of early history. The bourgeois was originally like the worker, an anxious toiler, though his work was of a different kind; the only source of his successfulness was the value of his work, his painstaking industry, and his careful application: capital by itself is no justification of a man. The way in which the bourgeois at their beginnings cut themselves clear and at the same time improved their position seems to indicate less the evolution of a particular class than the success of individuals due to their own personal qualities. The quality of a bourgeois (what he is, not what he has) is altogether determined by his work, and that is why he seems still to belong among the working-people; he is first cousin to the worker, and any worker can become a bourgeois, who is, in fact, simply a worker who was born to "get on." This can be seen very

clearly in the United States, where the bourgeoisie is the
least traditional that there is. But why then is there such
fierce hostility between the bourgeoisie and the working
class? Why should they be the chief antagonists in the
warfare of capitalist society?

The bourgeois betrayed the working people for, issuing
from their midst, he soon showed greater enterprise and
energy. And it was bound to be so, for mediæval man could
not subsist for ever. A new world appeared in which an
appetite for universal hegemony had made itself felt; Dr.
Faustus arose, and his principle was manifested in the bourgeoisie. They were not content to remain an organic part
of the working people, even as their leaders and vanguard.
They began to blush for their origin, clothed themselves
in frock coats and top hats, built expensive hotels, casinos,
and restaurants; they made a new class which was hostile to
the working people and organized an oppressive system of
employment for purposes of exploitation. It was a tragedy
in the moral order, and it led to all the fury and horrors
of the class war in capitalist society.

The theory that the bourgeoisie is nothing else than
a qualitative selection of the most gifted and that the
whole working class has remained at a lower level because
of its inefficiency is both false and cynical. There is, in
fact, among the bourgeois a huge number of untalented
and incapable people of a low type occupying important and responsible positions, just as there are extremely
gifted workers of a very high type. Only genius, that
divine gift, or a very exceptional ability can make its way
through all and every difficulty and obstacle. But genius
is not bourgeois.

The bourgeois refuses to see his work in its aspect as a
part of the service of mankind and has been the principal

contributor to the "atomization" of human society; he has established the principle and fact of economic competition, with its pitiless selfishness, and put all his money on the power of force. He has exalted the development of material economic resources above man and above the soul of man.

It is interesting to notice that Marx glorified and idealized the bourgeoisie at the same time that he hated it, precisely because, as I have already said, he taught that it had the great mission of developing productive material forces and so making Socialism possible; therefore he implicitly approved its betrayal of the working people, because that paved the way for the formation of the proletariat. Historically, bourgeois activities have led to an accumulation of ill-feeling and downright hatred; they produced conditions of work which were more inhuman than those of serfdom and which cannot possibly be justified in the conscience of a Christian; economic uncertainty and anxiety, the absence of all guarantee of day-today security, have reached their limit under Capitalism. This general disorder has embittered men and thrown them into a fiendish chaos; man has freed himself from subjection to natural necessity only to fall under the power of a fictitious rule of money in which it is impossible to identify realities. But the conflict between the bourgeois and the worker, now more acute than ever before, raises the question of the bourgeois spirit, an altogether special phenomenon to be distinguished from social "bourgeoisism" and not necessarily anything to do with a class.

This spirit in itself is apart from the strife of bourgeoisie and proletariat, Capitalism and Socialism. It is not a product of Capitalism (it was in existence long before), but Capitalism strengthened and consolidated it, and proletarians and socialists are easily infected with it. It has bred materialism, "economicism," the worship of material success, the denial of the spiritual world and of a future life. Everything is imprisoned by fixed limits, infinity is shut up within the soul — in other words, the very souls of men are made bourgeois.

Léon Bloy passionately indicted the bourgeois spirit in his profoundly acute book *Exégèse des lieux communs*. He was a Catholic, belonging to the generation of the French Symbolists, and he neither understood Socialism nor knew anything about Marx's theory of the proletariat; but he was most powerful in condemnation of Capitalism and the rule of Mammon as a betrayal of Christ (whom he always refers to as *le Pauvre*). He defended the cause of the destitute and suffering, sang their praise and revealed the mystery of money which, by the crucifixion, set apart the Poor Man from worldly wealth. For Bloy, the bourgeois, believing only in visible things and handing eternity over to time, is the destroyer of Paradise. He is definite that it is Christianity, not Socialism and the proletariat, that is radically opposed to "bourgeoisism," though aware all the time that there is, alas, such a thing as bourgeois Christianity, bourgeois Catholicism — and that he abhors more than anything else. He observes bitterly that the Lord God is looked on as very decorative in the shops of the bourgeois.

There is no correspondence between Bloy and the classification of the Marxist scheme, but he would probably have found plenty of examples of bourgeois wisdom among the communists, for the communist is the perfected bourgeois who has won his final victory and become collective man embracing the whole earth. Socialism is free from the bourgeois spirit only during its short period of nihilistic and devilish destructiveness while its revolutionary *pathos* lasts. The socialist and communist ideal of man is the same as that of the bourgeois, "economic man," who, without personality and soul, is exclusively concerned with the technical organization of life. The result is that Socialism, having no spiritual basis, has no idea of human personality, for the ideal of "comrade" does not correspond in the least to that of "man". It has reference only to the social relations existing between creatures. The dismal paradise of an hygienic factory is an essentially bourgeois ideal.

I have cited Léon Bloy, but besides him there was a whole pleiad of gifted thinkers and writers in the nine-teenth century (*the* capitalist century) who rose against the bourgeois spirit and attacked it vigorously; and they were not proletarians or supporters of any socialist move-ment. I name only Thomas Carlyle, Kierkegaard, Ibsen, Nietzsche, and in Russia, Tolstoi, Dostoievsky, Fedorov, and the reactionary Leontiev. This category of hostility towards "bourgeoisism" was created by the Romantics; and the importance of Symbolism lay in its refusal to put up with the bourgeois spirit, which it threw aside rather than fought against. All these are spiritual phenomena incidental to the conflict between the proletariat and the bourgeoisie, evidence that we are faced with a problem that is spiritual as well as social; and in fact the task of overcoming "bourgeoisism" is more than a social under-taking, and we are on the eve of a very serious conflict of the spirit. Socialism and Communism do not understand this, and they continue to fight the battle on economic and "class" grounds, without taking into account that they are already in subjection to their adversary. Spirit excludes "bourgeoisism" and all denial of spirit is in a measure indicative of a bourgeois mentality. "Bourgeoi-sism" is at the opposite pole to authentic and integral

Christianity, that is, to the religion of the Cross; it is a negation of that Cross and of the tragic principle in life. The worker, corrupted by a shameless demagogy and with all notion of sin rooted out of his soul, may well become bourgeois and an exploiter in his hour of triumph; when he is master he may persecute the intellectual among his fellow proletarians and exterminate all spiritual aristocracy.

From these conclusions we may determine the Christian estimate of the social movements going on in the world, and the attitude of Christianity towards class war. Christian consciousness, being rooted in the spiritual world, cannot be determined by this war, it must necessarily rise above it, and in consequence alone can judge it; Christianity draws its judgements of value from a deeper source than material economic life, from spiritual life and the revelation of the higher world. The class war exists and we must admit that a truth, even if only a partial one, rests with one or other or both of the combatants. We assume that there is more truth on the side of the workers. But the spiritual state of the parties is more important for us than their economic situation. Our business is not only to overcome bourgeois relations between men, relations which reach their ultimate expression in capitalist society, but also to overcome the bourgeois attitude towards life. Now to overcome this "bourgeoisism" of the soul the first and most important thing to do is to accept the mystery of the Cross.

The social problem cannot be solved apart from the spiritual problem; unless there is a Christian renewal of souls, those of the workers above all, the sway of Socialism will become definitively a domination by the bourgeois spirit — to the satisfaction of this world and a denial of eternity. The quest of the Kingdom of God alone can

lead to victory. The ennobling of society, that is to say, its
permeation by a spiritual aristocracy, ought to be at least
on a level with its democratization; the new society will
be a society of workers, and it must have an aristocratic
principle. It must not repudiate all hierarchy, in accordance
with the mechanical conception of the world, but display
the authentic human hierarchy of qualities, talents, and
callings; that we must rise above classes and put a brake
on their strife does not mean that the distribution of
work according to diversity of gifts must be done away
with, and an anti-hierarchical principle of mechanical
uniformity established. In practice the communists recognise this clearly enough, but they refuse on principle to
admit the presence of an aristocratic element in spiritual
culture; they are ready to accept political and economic
inequality by force of external necessity, but they enforce a
uniform levelling-down of spiritual culture, the subjection
of quality to quantity.

But outside religion the contradiction of the aristocratic
principle is insurmountable. Christianity alone can show
the way out of the difficulty, for it recognizes a spiritual
nobility, the aristocracy of the sons of God, independent
of men's social position. Aristocracy based on privilege
has a Greco-Roman, that is to say pagan, origin, and apart
from Christianity it is threatened by futility and barbarism.
The state of the Christian soul is conditioned by a sense
of transgression committed and not of injury received.
Now the consciousness of blameworthiness in respect of
sin is, spiritually speaking, a nobler and more aristocratic
condition than a feeling of injuredness, and only Christianity cures the human soul of this mean susceptibility
that breeds jealousy and ill-feeling. There is nothing more
painful today than to watch the irreparable decline of

human culture, to see it overwhelmed by mere quantity; the unavoidable process of our time deals it blow after blow till it is threatened with total extinction, and that process can be controlled only by religion, by a spiritual effort of the people at large.

It is most important that it should be understood that Christianity does not and cannot form its estimates of Capitalism and Socialism from an evolutionary standpoint. A Christian cannot follow the Russian Marxists of the end of the last century and regard Capitalism on the one hand as an evil to be fought and on the other as a thing to be encouraged, because its expansion will widen the gulf between the classes, develop productive forces, and provoke the proletariat to yet greater hatred. Such relativism only raises an unsolvable moral antinomy. One may think industrial and economic progress a good and valuable thing, and consequently be in favour of it. Just so Russian Communism today accelerates industrialization at the expense of the Capitalism which it repudiates (though Communism itself is exposed to moral condemnation). But I may not approve what I believe to be wicked and unjust. I can affirm a positive value in an element of Capitalism associated with material development today as well as yesterday, but if there was an essential injustice in it in the past, it will be there also in the future, and that I must reject. I may not encourage people to consent to it even temporarily, for good can be born only out of good, never out of evil. The wickedness and injustice of Capitalism are not lessened by the degree of its development or by the benefits which it confers, and Christianity can judge its spiritual and moral shortcomings only by reference to eternal things, the spiritual and moral fundamentals of society. Marxism allows that the souls and bodies of men may be sacrificed in the interests of economic prosperity; Christianity allows no such thing.

There is no reason to suppose that economic development is possible only on immoral principles which overturn the foundations of life, and call for the unloosing of a greedy selfishness and other sinful passions which for the Christian can be matters only of avoidance or of repentance; it can have another basis than unscrupulous competition, namely the "community of action" in the sense in which N. F. Fedorov understood it.[4]

---

[4] N. F. Fedorov's *Philosophy of Common Work* consisted in the union of all human forces — scientific, economic, social, national and international — for one great task: the victory over nature and the defeat of death. [TR.]

CHAPTER VI

The Church & the New Social Reality • Man &
Class • The Social Problem as a Spiritual Problem

THE WHOLE TENOR OF OUR CON-
siderations points to the conclusion that Christianity cannot abstain from making a practical
judgement in this matter of class war; Christians must
not content themselves with the statement that nothing
has happened since the days of the Fathers, feigning ignorance of the existence of a new social reality. Christian
consciousness is in fact behind the times where present-
day social and cultural processes are concerned, a proof
of the degeneration of modern Christianity and its lack
of creative enterprise. The Church, considered historically
and externally, seems to be indifferent to the astonishing
changes that have taken place in the world; she does not
seem to have noticed that the patriarchal conditions which
she envisages no longer exist and that entirely fresh social
relations are now operative, but she cannot much longer
escape the necessity of determining her attitude towards
this new social reality. Sooner or later she will have to pro-
nounce from the depths of her consciousness in favour of
one or other of the protagonists and definitely take sides.[1]

---

[1] M. Berdyaev seems to have in mind *primarily* the Eastern

The preaching of St. John Chrysostom corresponded with contemporaneous social reality, and that was a sort of communism, in no wise analogous to conditions in a capitalist epoch. The Church's exhortations urge us to solve the social problem by means of mercy and alms-deeds, and, in spite of the rhetoric, hardened hearts are sometimes touched by them; but today they fall far short of the actual facts and are quite inadequate to the requirements of the campaign for social justice; they are the voice of a past that is dead and gone. In particular, the categories of social thought and speech of the Russian Orthodox Church are still entirely adapted to a former organization of society; anyone would think that we still lived in the world of the nobles and peasants and merchants and *petits bourgeois*, as if not only the proletarian revolution, but even the bourgeois revolution had never happened. The Church looks towards eternity, but she also lives in time, and must speak a social language that is suited to the world which she addresses. It was so in past ages. But today her speech is archaic and applicable only to conditions of which but few traces remain. The social basis of the Church is changing and the new one must be formed principally of workers, with a minority of intellectuals; no more nobles, no more of the old commercial class. The society of the future will be a working society, and the Church will be able to live in accordance therewith as she did with the societies of the past, continuing to be the guardian of the eternal truths which she offers to the souls of mankind.

It is a monstrous statement, supremely contrary to the Christian spirit but upheld by some reactionaries, that

Orthodox Church of which he is a member. But his strictures are applicable in varying lesser degrees to the authorities of all the historical Christian churches. [TR.]

the Church normally can live only in a patriarchal society that is monarchical and divided into castes, that she ought to shun this working society that has overturned ranks and classes, refuse it her blessing, and take refuge in the wilderness. In reality, the Christian Church must at this time be specially solicitous for the workers, because, having conquered in the social order, they are now threatened spiritually by the greatest dangers and are being infected by the deadly poison of godlessness. The true Church of Christ has never been corrupted by worldly interests and knows nothing of classes; when a man comes to her in quest of spiritual food and eternal life he ceases to be noble or plebeian, bourgeois or proletarian, all fading honours and vanities are cast aside, for no attribute of caste or class has any value in the eyes of God. And if the Orthodox Church has particularly favoured the imperial and terri-torial nobility and her hierarchs have had a weakness for the great ones of the earth, this was not of God, but of Caesar; a tribute paid to this world, a pandering to "the spirit of the age." In the depths of her consciousness the Church in the beginning transcended and excluded classes, there are still no such things so far as she is concerned. If we rise above the class hatred that torments the world we thereby rise spiritually and morally above the classes themselves and the spirit that informs them. Marx knew nothing of such a triumph; he recognized a privileged class, preached a class attitude among men, and welcomed the fury and hatred that follow therefrom.

When we speak of rising above this hatred we do not mean that the Church should advocate a reconciliation of the classes based on the submissiveness of those who are oppressed and exploited. This would be the sheer-est hypocrisy and would brand the Church for ever as bourgeois. War is not simply an evil; it may be a good as well, and one demanded by the proper dignity of man. It is altogether wrong to preach humility to the exploited when it is clearly to the exploiters that these counsels should be addressed; moreover, humility is not a social act, but a private and spiritual one. It is the Church's duty to condemn the oppression and exploitation of man by man primarily on moral and spiritual grounds and not in the name of some social system; she must give her blessing to the search for a more equitable and humane regime and entrust the struggle for a better future to man's own enterprise, activity, and freedom. Social conflict is inevitable and will come about whatever else happens. It is not the business of Christianity to settle the technique and methods of this conflict, but to form the spiritual and moral atmosphere of the souls who are engaged in it and to fight against that sinfulness which breeds a devilish rancour. Gandhi is not a Christian, but his "passive resistance," his inoffensive war, are far more in accordance with the spirit of Christianity than are the methods to which so-called Christian societies so often have recourse.

Christian consciousness must first of all make a sharp distinction between its attitude towards individual men and towards a class, a distinction between what is deeper, primary, and concerned with eternity and what is secondary and temporal. Man, not class, is the heir to eternal life; class is "something afar off," man is our neighbour. All classes are levelled out in the face of death and eternity; man alone remains. This truth must be learned by the "proletariat" as well as by the "bourgeoisie." Our fundamental business is this of *Man and of Class*. If Christianity takes sides with the working class in the social struggle she does not do so in the name of that class; it is in the name of man, of the dignity of the workman, in the name of his human rights and of his soul which Capitalism so grievously grinds down. There is a lot of difference between this and materialistic Socialism; if there is something of socialism in it, it is nevertheless strictly "personalist": Christianity leads to individualization rather than to collectivization. The machine, which has created Capitalism, makes everything collective and impersonal; but it is possible that a further development of technique will give us machines that will encourage the contrary process, and then "impersonalism," inherent alike in Capitalism and Communism, will disappear. Proudhon may yet conquer Marx. But Christianity does not require individualization only, it also calls for the conquest of individualism on behalf of the brotherhood of men.

Up till now Christianity has been helpless before the crushing reality of the class war, with which she had no corresponding previous experience, and her task indeed presents a very complex duality. It is less a matter of deciding on which side truth lies than of knowing how to dispel the feelings of hatred that imbue the holders of the truth. The Church can bless the struggle against the tyranny and exploitation used by the bourgeois as a social class, but she cannot bless hatred of that class and all its members, whereas this animosity is part of the morality of materialistic Socialism and still more of that Communism in which man is quite swallowed up by class. How are the workers to be delivered from these devilish emotions to which Marx attributed a messianic importance?

The ordinary preaching of Christian virtues, love, humility, mercy, is barren and without effect; it is often even dismissed as conventional rhetoric, hypocrisy, a concealed attempt to weaken and disarm the enemy. It is, however, also true that communist "preaching" has quickly become a matter of exasperating platitudes, full of the conventional rhetoric of the demagogue. A very grave responsibility rests with us Christians. Our times call for speech that is charged with freshness, youthful vigour, creative energy — and we have not yet found it; the usual exhortation to humility rings false in this atmosphere of social wrongs. The soul of the worker has been contaminated by the poisons given off by Capitalism and class war, and it is extremely difficult to bring it to an understanding of Christian truth. To do this successfully it is needful that Christianity present itself to the mind of the worker as associated with social truth, and not with social falsehood. In other words, Christians ought to be on the side of work and the workers.

A new estimate of the social obligations of Christianity has made its appearance among the younger generations of Europeans, both Catholic and Protestant, and the best and more intelligent among them are definitely against Capitalism and the bourgeois spirit. That is an encouraging sign. These ideas are still very weak among the young Orthodox Russians, who do not understand the religious importance of the social problem and have not yet got rid of their negative reactions to Communism. But while one part of the youth of Europe is fascinated by this problem and the religious approach thereto, another part gives its enthusiasm to national and racial questions, as do, for example, the young fascists and the German national-socialists. The world is split by two equally atrocious quarrels, between classes and between nations, and together they threaten the unity of the whole human race.

Marx, betrayed by his monistic economic method, did not properly understand the significance of national and

racial wars; for him they were entirely dependent on economic processes, although actually the national element
has considerable importance, positive and negative. But
while Socialism and its class war looks towards the future,
nationalism, though still able to influence the present,
is no more than a heritage from the past. Only among
Eastern peoples is nationalism also looking forward, and
with them it is, by comparison with European Capitalism,
still a social reality. Generally speaking, nationalism is as
prolific of hatred and hostility as the class war, and it has
no thought for a future free from such angry strife. Racial-
ism, whatever its cause, is an eminently anti-Christian
phenomenon, and the religious forms it sometimes takes
can only be regarded as an ebullition of paganism; the
fascists and the Hitlerites are pagans and enemies of Christ.
As for the nationalism drawn from Orthodox sources — a
very old complaint — that is pagan too, a perversion of
Christianity and of the Orthodox Church.

The Christian condemnation of nationalism and
particularism is not a denial of nationality, of national
feeling and achievement, of love of one's people, nor is
it prompted by an abstract internationalism or a rejec-
tion of patriotism. But the great Christian and human
mission of our time is for the union and conciliation of
all peoples, the attainment, not of an international and
abstract unity, but of a supranational concrete unity of
mankind. Nationalist and particularist movements are
a huge obstacle in the way of the solution of the social
question; they increase the proportion of enmity in the
world, and they result in a primitive and coarse natu-
ralism every bit as hostile to spirit and spirituality as is
materialistic Communism. But this problem is incidental to my subject, and I cannot here make any adequate

analysis of it. I will only say that the problem of class
conflict is really intimately bound up with that of military war, the most horrifying danger that threatens
us. We have good reasons for the statement that every
national war between states would become a social war
between classes.[2] This would be the bloody and agonizing
end of Capitalism, and no nation could emerge victori-
ous; it is more than possible that then would be heard
the death-knell of European culture.

Nationalists and bourgeois partizans make a plausible
charge against the workers that they selfishly put their
own class interests above the interests of the nation and
of the state. Inwardly and morally the position is not so
simple as that. The workers are justifiably suspicious that
the financial and international (called national) politics
in whose name they are called on to make such sacrifices
may hide a bankers' ramp; it is undeniable that it often
does. The workers' unions have the right to oppose fiscal
politics and its "rationalization" of industry that means
more unemployment, and to stand out against a war bred
by a mad conflict of financial interests. If the workers had
had the strength to refuse to co-operate in world-wide war
they would have brought an enormous benefit to mankind
and to every nation — and that is not at all equivalent to
denying the existence of state and national interests that
are real and lawful.

Christianity will never accept the abolition of man's
personal conscience, reason, and freedom, or approve their
substitution by a class conscience, reason and freedom; a
universal reason it knows, but not a class reason. I must
repeat that man is a deeper and higher reality than race

---

[2] See the interesting work of the syndicalist Edouard Berth, *Guerre
des Etats ou guerre des classes*.

or class, and this truth must be upheld against all classes and all their interests and hates.

In the nineteenth century, men of an idealist spirit, thirsting for justice, tried to spiritualize and ennoble the bourgeois controlling classes, urging them to unselfishness and sacrifice. They thought it might help to preach to them as a moral truth that the worker also is a man and that human dignity must be respected even in the lower classes. So in times past had men taught concerning slaves and serfs. But we have reached a time when the old forms of moral persuasion no longer correspond with the actual conditions; they are outmoded and will not henceforward suffice. The task before us now is to spiritualize and ennoble, not the bourgeoisie whose moral importance is irretrievably lost, but the working class, whose social significance and power are daily increasing and will be of yet greater weight in the future. It is demonstrably too late to ask the bourgeoisie to make sacrifices; it is now a matter of teaching the workers that the bourgeois and the gentleman also are human beings, that they must be treated accordingly and their dignity and worth respected. This, at least, is the position in Soviet Russia, and the same will probably come about one day in the West.

We must deny before God and man that one's attitude towards men may be determined solely by considering them as representatives of this or that class. Let us say, for example, that M. Poincaré's politics were a bourgeois policy sheltering capitalist interests; that was my personal opinion and it alienated my sympathy from him. But it is impossible to determine my whole attitude towards Poincaré simply by that consideration. I must take into account the fact that he is a very cultured man, sincerely patriotic, and of an irreproachable integrity. And the same attitude must be adopted when it is a question of Stalin, of anybody else, of men in general.

Every man is made in the image of God, however indistinct that image may become, and every man is called to eternal life; in the face of these truths, all differentiation by class, all political passion, all the superfluities that social life piles daily on the human soul are trivial and unavailing. That is why the problem of the class war, important as it is economically, juridically, and technically, is above all a spiritual and moral problem, involving a new attitude of Christians towards man and society and a religious renewal of all mankind.